LEAVING YOUR *Lover*

They have left

the path of truth...

DEB GORMAN

Leaving Your Lover

Copyright 2018 Deb Gorman
All rights reserved

Unless otherwise indicated, all Scripture quotations are taken from the Holy Bible, New Living Translation, copyright © 1996, 2004, 2007 by Tyndale House Foundation. Used by permission of Tyndale House Publishers, Inc., Carol Stream, Illinois 60188. All rights reserved.

Edited by Dori Harrell, Breakout Editing
Cover design by Emilie Hendryx
Author's photograph by Ric Brunstetter, RBIII Studios
Formatting by Colleen Jones, Colleen's Committed Collaborations

ISBN 978-0-9979587-5-1 (Paperback)
ISBN 978-0-9979587-4-4 (Digital)

Published by Deb Gorman
Debo Publishing
www.debggorman.com

To our children: Stacie, Nicole, Shellie, Chad, Jessica, Chris, and Sarah, and their children.
May the path I walk today lead you to the Lover of your souls.

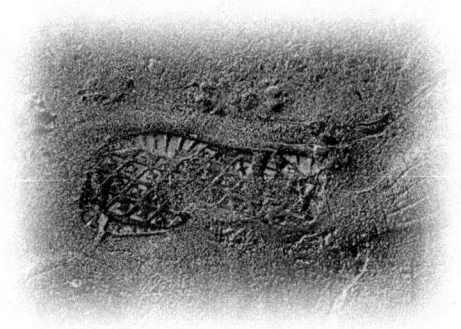

Acknowledgments

To Jesus the Christ, who fashioned me just the way he wanted and breathed his Spirit into me when I was fourteen. In fifty years of walking with him, he has never left my side, never let me down, and never lied to me—although I have done all those things to him. He is forever faithful, forever full of grace and mercy, and forever mine. Jesus, my Friend, I can't wait to jump into your arms when I reach your door. May the time be short, and may I spend it for you.

To my husband, Alan, who consistently tells me the truth and puts up with my myriad idiosyncrasies. He is truly, simply, the best man I have ever met, and I'm looking forward to the next thirty years with you at my side.

To all of my friends, coworkers, family members, and even perfect strangers who have endured those nosy characters who pop out of my imagination and interrupt conversations, ask impertinent questions, and generally make themselves obnoxious. Thank you for understanding that I have absolutely no control over them—they come and go as they please.

To those bookish professionals who mentor me in my writing and publishing journey, I simply can't say thank you enough. My editor, Dori Harrell; my cover designer, Emilie Hendryx; the friends and teachers I've met at conferences—all of *you* live between the lines and pages of this book. There are many more—and I thank you in my heart.

And last but certainly not least, thank you to you—the reader. I pray that Jesus reaches beyond my poor words and touches you, allowing you to experience his glory, majesty, grace, and His humanity. He loves us more than we will ever know.

Contents

Introduction	1
Chapter 1 Snake in the Grass	3
Chapter 2 Offering	19
Chapter 3 The Lie	41
Chapter 4 For a Mess of Pottage	55
Chapter 5 Eye Spy	65
Chapter 6 Samson and the Spy	77
Chapter 7 Bleat	93
Chapter 8 Fallen	103
Chapter 9 As the Heart Turns	117
Chapter 10 Whisper	131
Chapter 11 Swallowed	147
Chapter 12 The Kiss	161
Chapter 13 Root	185

Introduction

As the song lyrics go, there are innumerable ways to leave those who care about us.

Kids leave home, with or without Mom and Dad's blessing. Spouses get fed up and hit the road, looking for greener pastures. Churches split over minutiae. We quit our jobs, we leave neighborhoods in which we've lived for decades, and worst of all, some depart this world by their own hand, leaving a trail of broken hearts, unmendable by anything this world has to offer. Yes, there are many ways to leave—whatever or whomever we feel we must abandon.

God's Word brims with people who left the Lover of their souls, and he put their stories into the Scriptures for a reason—and the reason is us and all who come after.

Each left the path of God, some only for a short time before coming to their senses. But some left permanently even after tasting his goodness. Some of these tales will break your heart, but some will have you cheering at the end because he or she came back to the great romance.

These stories are about biblical characters—real flesh-and-blood people—who lived and died from creation to the first century. I've expanded on them, remaining true to each biblical account but filling in details in order to help us see, feel, taste, and smell the crucial events of their lives. In this way, imagining what it could have been like for Jonah to be swallowed by a great sea creature, or for Judas Iscariot to kiss the cheek of Jesus, we can learn how their ancient stories intersect with our own.

I hope you enjoy their stories. I hope their stories make you think—and I hope you allow God to reveal your story to you.

~Deb Gorman

Chapter 1
Snake in the Grass

And you will be like God, knowing good and evil.
~Genesis 3:5

Adam peeked through the leaves of the massive tree. Moisture from the early morning dew dripped off the leaves, wetting his cheeks. What was Father doing there in the clearing? Adam changed positions, carefully climbing up to the next branch so he could see better.

The Lord God scooped dirt in his large hands and gently brushed it and patted it down, making a mounded border around the perimeter of an oblong depression he'd made in the ground. Adam judged he could just about stretch out in it—his feet might hang over the end a bit. From a pile of rushes nearby, Father carried an armful and carefully arranged it over the mound of dirt, piling it up a bit over the raised border. Adam thought it looked like a resting place. Was the Creator making a bed for himself? He shook his head in wonder—he'd never seen the Lord God sleep. Did he? Adam looked from the newly created bower to the form of his Father and shook his head. Father was much taller than himself. He'd never fit into it.

Father stepped back and looked at his handiwork, muscled arms folded in front of him, one finger on his chin. The small flowers at his feet bowed their tiny white faces to the ground. He looked down and murmured something to them that Adam couldn't hear. Whatever he said made them look up again, their miniature faces gleaming in joy. Adam could have sworn their leafy hands were clapping.

"Adam, son, you can come down now," Father said quietly, not turning around.

Adam sighed. He could never hide from Father for long, try as he might. They'd played hide-and-seek before, finding new hiding places with each game, shouting gleefully when the seeker found the hider. But he could never win against Father—although he *allowed* him to win sometimes. Adam suspected Father liked playing the game as much as he did, so Father allowed Adam a small victory from time to time.

He slid down the smooth branches and jumped off the bottom one, his feet almost landing on a stand of beautiful tulips. He managed to avoid them at the last minute and landed in a heap next to them. He jumped to his feet and apologized to the regal red petals. They dipped their heads in acknowledgment. Adam stepped hesitantly to Father's side.

"What is it, Father? Why do you make a resting place?"

Father, his countenance glowing like the sun, laughed as he took Adam's face between his palms.

"It's not a resting place, my son. It's a creating place," he said, tenderly brushing a smudge of soil from Adam's face.

Adam looked at the nest, then back at Father, who laughed out loud.

"You should see your face—I can tell you have a thousand questions!"

"But, Father, another creation? I thought you were finished. All those trees and plants and animals—and bugs and birds and bacterium and—and I named every one of them! What more could we possibly need here? Everything is already perfect in this place."

Father didn't answer—just watched Adam's face. Adam gazed back at him, puzzled. There'd never been a time when he'd been confused at Father's actions. They'd always had perfect intimacy between them, ever since he'd heard Father call his

name and he opened his eyes to see Father's face inches from his own, eyes crinkled up as he threw his head back and laughed joyfully. Father's voice was the first sound Adam had ever heard, and he'd never get over loving it.

Adam turned his head, his eyes roaming the riotous color of the surrounding flowering hedges and the huge trees spreading their branches in a canopy above them. Miniature daisies, their yellow and white faces now smiling skyward, dotted the cool green of the grass at his feet. He breathed deeply of their scent. The cacophony of chattering birds overhead, calling good morning to each other, lent a joyful backdrop. He'd explored this garden since the day—how long ago was it?—he'd awakened to that lovely voice in his ear. Each adventure revealed a new reason to love Father, a new facet of his character to wonder at. Adam knew Eden was created just for him, and he fit into it like clear water in a cupped leaf.

Curiously though, Adam sensed something missing for the first time. He frowned, shading his eyes as he looked into the distance. He saw the antelope playing on the wooded hills across the wide river that meandered over the landscape to the south. They danced and leaped over each other, playing like…what? Some lay near the river with their young, their parents basking peacefully in each other's presence.

He looked up to the nearest tree, an enormous oak with limbs wide enough to sleep on. Perched up there among the leaves were two tiny bluebirds chirping, heads bobbing up and down. Adam couldn't make out what they were saying, but it seemed a lovely, lively conversation. The male leaned over and rubbed his head on his mate's tiny wing.

His gaze traveled lower, and he saw two squirrels peering at him from their tiny den, secluded among the foliage.

Adam rubbed his forehead with his hand. An unknown curious feeling assailed his senses. He couldn't name it. He turned his head and saw that Father observed him intently, a gentle smile on his face. Father then grinned wide and clapped him on the shoulder.

"You'll see, my son. You'll see. It'll be the best of all. I promise. Now, I'd like you to help me gather some flowers. We must make it very special. It must be...pretty. Yes," he murmured, "she'll want it to be pretty."

"Pretty? What's *pretty*, Father?" Adam didn't recall ever hearing that word.

"You'll have to be patient, Adam. I promise you—you'll understand the word soon enough."

Adam shrugged, content to wait. Father had never broken a promise—indeed, the word *broken* wasn't even a part of Adam's language—anything that *broke* in Eden remade itself instantly, such was Father's power.

They busied themselves sticking flowers in the rushes and around the edges of the nest. As soon as the blooms left the hand for their new home, they rooted and flowered again. Adam picked some spicy-scented herbs that smelled pleasant and scattered them throughout the rushes.

The Lord God put the last sprig of daisy just so, and they stepped back, standing arm in arm to survey their work.

"Yes, my son, it's perfect. We are ready to begin."

"Begin?" Adam asked curiously. He walked away, stopping to face Father from the other side of the cradle. "Begin what?"

Father beckoned Adam to his side and touched his forehead gently. As he slipped to the ground, his Father's loving arms were strong around him as he gently laid him next to the sweet-smelling bower.

When Adam awoke again, his life in the garden of God was never the same. He raised himself up on one elbow, shaking the sleep out of his eyes. Father was kneeling and bending over the cradle on the ground next to him, blowing a steady stream of air from his mouth. A sudden sweet smell permeated the small clearing. The chattering of animals hushed, and the gentle breeze died down. The air seemed charged with excitement as Adam jumped to his feet and looked down.

When Adam saw the woman for the first time, he knew the *something missing* rested on the ground at his feet. He watched, hiding shyly behind Father, a smile playing around his lips as the Lord God whispered in her ear. She awakened and stretched. Father stood up and stepped back, gesturing to Adam.

"Here she is, my son. What do you think?"

Adam stepped closer and gazed into her eyes, seeing there what he'd not known was missing.

This creature is like me!

Then she smiled at him, and he was instantly captivated.

"At last!" he exclaimed joyfully. "This one is bone from my bone and flesh from my flesh! We will call her 'woman' because you fashioned her from me."

Adam knelt beside her and touched her cheek. The wonder in her eyes must surely match his own.

He heard a low voice in his mind, then a giggle.

You are Adam. He told me—and that I am for you.

She speaks to me!

Yes of course, silly!

She heard my thought...I cannot speak like this to his other creatures.

No, only to me, Adam. But what is that behind you, the creature with no legs spreading its arms and hands to the...blue roof? She struggled with the descriptive words.

Adam looked behind him at the tree he'd climbed just a short time ago.

Tree.

Tree? It's a pretty name.

Adam caught his breath. *Pretty. Father had used that word. Yes, now I know what "pretty" is.*

You are Eve.

"Eve?" She tried the word with her new voice.

"Your name is Eve, for you will be the mother of all who come after us."

He heard a rustle in the hedge to the left and looked just in time to see Father disappearing, chuckling gently to himself.

He turned his attention back to the woman. They gazed into each other's eyes, complete knowledge swallowing them whole, surrounding them as their thoughts mingled and flowed together, merging like small creeks into the mighty river.

Her girlish giggle was infectious, enchanting. He giggled with her, which made her break into peals of laughter. Soon they were both on their backs, laughing at the sky, tears running into their ears. He sat up and took her hand in his, turning it over, separating each finger gently. Her hand was so small compared to his, but there was strength there—he could feel it.

Adam suddenly jumped to his feet and pulled Eve up. She was a bit unsteady, like a new foal on its legs for the first time. But soon she walked around the small space with ease, touching leaves and bending over to sniff blossoms. She hesitantly put out a hand to touch the head of a hare that had appeared from its hole in the foliage. As she petted its head, she turned a rapturous gaze on Adam.

"Hare. He's called hare," Adam said.

"He's beautiful. His feet are so large compared to the rest of him." The more she spoke out loud, the clearer her words became.

"Just wait until you see what he can do with those feet."

The hare's mate appeared, scolding him, sending Eve into fits of giggling again. The female hare pushed her erring mate into the foliage, throwing a backward glance at Eve. Eve waved her fingers at her, but the hare just harrumphed and ducked into the opening and disappeared. Adam took her hand again and pulled her to the edge of the clearing.

"Come on, Eve! I want to show you everything!"

She nodded and slipped out of his grasp, first walking, then trotting, then running like a gazelle toward the river. She looked back at him.

"Catch me if you can, Adam!"

He laughed and ran after her. The next adventure was upon him.

***

"Eve, my love! Where are you?" Adam had searched everywhere for her, even swimming across the river to her special place. She liked to lay in the sun on a wide, flat rock and watch the antelope and zebras cavort with each other. She wasn't there though, so he walked along the river, calling her name. She'd always answered him when he called. He wasn't worried—the garden of God was safe.

Safe? Curious word. I've never even thought to use it.

Adam finally gave up looking for her and made his way back to their home under the trees.

When he arrived, the place was unnaturally quiet for this time of day. Usually Eve was there, humming while she prepared the evening meal, but she was nowhere to be found. He decided he'd surprise her with her favorite meal—the root that grew nearby was delicious when barely cooked and served with the lettuces they'd taught themselves to cultivate. The sun Father had created was not yet set. Adam waved at the shining sphere hovering over the far mountains, and the sun waved back, scattering shimmers of golden light on the hills.

Adam busied himself with supper, surprised that Eve had not yet returned. He put the food on the rock they used for a table and sat down to wait. When he could wait no longer, he finally ate. As he was finishing, he heard Father's voice.

"My son, where is the woman?" Father walked into the clearing.

"I don't know, Father. Don't you?" Father always knew.

"Go find her, Adam. She needs you."

"But—"

"Go find her."

Adam jumped to his feet and charged out of the clearing, calling her name. He heard no response. He searched in concentric circles, with their home as the center. He walked rapidly in ever-widening rounds, calling her name, looking in caves and in bushes and trees. He even asked the animals he encountered to look for her. Nothing.

Finally, he came to the small clearing in the middle of the garden, enclosed by large hedges with the huge spreading tree in the center. Father had shown him the sacred place but warned him against entering and eating the fruit of the tree. He'd taken Eve here one day and given her the same warning. It was the only thing God had made that was forbidden to them.

He approached quietly, surprised to hear voices. He parted the hedge and peered through. Eve stood with her back to him, holding something in her hands that he couldn't see.

Why is Eve here, and what is she holding? And whose voice is that?

Adam stood still and listened. The low, silky voice floated over her head to him. She moved slightly, and the creature who spoke came into view. Adam gasped.

Beautiful!

The serpent stood in front of her, his head inches from her face. His scaly skin glowed like the sun, sparkling in the dimness of the clearing. His large eyes gazed dreamily into Eve's as he spoke. The intimacy and beauty between them overpowered Adam's senses. He should do something though—he could still hear Father's voice in his head.

She needs you.

Still, he was loath to interrupt the scene. He waited a moment longer, his curiosity mounting.

The serpent's voice flowed on, cajoling her. His voice was curiously comforting, almost lulling Adam. Eve shook her head a few times, but the creature patiently persuaded, his deep, smooth voice like the purr of the giant cats who inhabited the heights.

"Daughter, you won't die! What a silly notion. What is death anyway?"

Daughter? The serpent isn't her father…

"God knows that your eyes will be opened as soon as you eat it, and you will be like him, knowing both good and evil."

Adam now saw what she held—a small fruit, glittering like a jewel in her hand. Eve held her hand up in front of her. She turned the fruit around slowly and watched it sparkle, throwing its light on the foliage around her. It was mesmerizing.

Surely not! his mind screamed.

Adam stepped back and found the path leading in, breaking through the hedge quietly.

At the last moment, before Adam could speak, she brought the fruit to her lips and took a small bite. She chewed noisily, allowing the juice to trickle down her chin. She hesitated, then took another bite.

"Daughter, we have company," the serpent said quietly.

Eve spun around. She looked uneasy.

Curious. There has never been uneasiness between us.

"Adam, my love," she said, the serpent's head now swaying over hers. "Come and meet my new…friend."

Adam took a step forward, then stopped. His eyes met the snake's. They were beautiful, more beautiful than any other creature's. A sound reached him—the snake was humming a low melody, one Adam had never heard. He glanced back at Eve. She nodded encouragingly. He took another step. She slowly lifted the hand that held the fruit. He hesitated.

It's forbidden!

But why did God forbid us, my love? Her thoughts spoke into his mind. *Is it because he's hiding its power from us? Look—I haven't been harmed.*

He saw that she hadn't—she looked the same as she always had, except for a tightness around her eyes and lips.

She advanced slowly toward him, still holding out the fruit. The serpent's song grew louder, now crashing through Adam's mind, drowning out everything else. He stretched out his hand, and she gently placed the fruit in his palm. It nestled there, cool and inviting. Its aroma assaulted his senses. He looked up and saw Eve waiting patiently, the snake peering intently above her head.

What could it hurt?

He brought the fruit to his lips and bit deeply—and felt the shift in his mind. It was as if he was instantly captured in a strange new dimension, wholly unfamiliar to him. He looked at Eve, the serpent, the tree, the fruit in his hand. Everything looked the same but somehow offbeat. He felt a frightening sensation in his chest, like a great hand squeezing his heart and lungs.

Fear.

Later that night, God found them, clinging to each other in desperation. They'd finally hidden themselves in the thick hedge surrounding their home after moving from place to place. But no niche seemed safe now—there was no hole deep enough, no tree high enough, no darkness thick enough to seclude them from the dread that enveloped them.

God approached and stood before them.

"My children, what is this you have done?"

***

Under the darkening sky, Adam and Eve waited for God to come back. They shivered in the cold night air. For the first time in their existence, they could not warm each other as their bodies clung together. The fig leaves they'd sewn for themselves, using a thorn plucked from a nearby hedge, did nothing to shield them from the unnatural chill. Adam had noted that when he picked the thorn, a new one had not immediately grown in its place.

Curious.

They heard screaming in the distance, joined by the howls, chirps, barks, and moans of other animals. They covered their ears, terrified at the unfamiliar voices. They'd never heard anything but joyful conversations between the animals, peppered with praise for their Creator—not this frightful disharmony spreading like a virus.

Eve grasped Adam tighter. "What's happening, husband?"

"I don't know. Tell me again what the serpent said just before you ate the fruit."

"You heard him," she retorted. "He said my eyes would be opened and I would be like God, knowing both good and evil."

Adam shook his head, a deep sadness spreading through his chest. There'd never once been discord between them.

"I think he lied. I think we now know evil by experience, but not as God does." He sat up suddenly, hearing the screams finally stop and the sound of a heavy tread nearby.

They jumped up, ready to face whatever was approaching on the other side of the hedge.

Father pushed through the brush. He was carrying something that dripped with moisture. Adam couldn't quite see what it was in the dim light, but he could smell it. Blood. He remembered the smell from a time when a sharp rock had sliced his foot. He'd been puzzled by the sight of the redness covering the bottom of his foot. He'd smelled it, curious. Father had been nearby and had explained what blood was, its properties, and that it was precious, life giving. Then he'd closed up the wound with his breath.

Father set animal skins tenderly on the ground and laid them out flat. He used a wide leaf to clean the blood and tissue. Adam and Eve crept out of the hedge and stood in shock. Eve leaned over to whisper in Adam's ear. "Adam, isn't that Aryeh? See the black pattern on the skin—there, on the belly? Isn't it her? What happened to her?" Eve wept softly.

Father rose and stood before them, delivering the harsh pronouncement. They were banished from their home. The serpent's legs disappeared, and he would forever crawl on his belly. The beloved animals would turn on each other. At that, Eve sank to the ground at Adam's feet. He touched the top of her head as he stood before his Creator.

I will not be weak.

"My son, you will be weak. Eve will desire to control you, but you will rule over her. Discord will be the result. You have already experienced it."

And on and on it went, each pronouncement harsher than the last. At the end, Father stooped to the ground and picked up Aryeh's skin.

"This is for you, Eve. Take off those leaves—they are inadequate. I will clothe you with this skin, and it will protect you from the harsh elements." She did as she was told, whimpering as the skin of her friend touched her nakedness. Father wrapped it around her and secured it with several long thorns.

Harsh elements?

"Yes, Adam. You will leave this place and never return. The animals will go with you—most of them. But they will not be as they were before."

"But, Father—"

"You listened to your wife and joined her in her disobedience. The ground is now cursed because of you. By the sweat of your brow you will till the ground. The animals, some of them, will now be your enemies, and you will have to kill them to eat. They will fear you and be unable to speak to you. Even your bodies have changed, my son. You will now need their meat to survive."

Adam could scarcely take it all in. He dropped to his knees beside Eve and wrapped his arms around her. She trembled in his arms, finally raising her head to look at his face. Shocked at what he saw, he couldn't speak.

Where is Eve? Who is this who has taken her place?

He used to be able to *see* Eve in her eyes, but a stranger now stared back. They used to be able to hear each other's thoughts, but now silence filled the spaces. Only emptiness existed between them, as if they were only hollowed-out shells—like Aryeh. Adam grasped her to his breast, and his tears mingled with hers.

Adam raised his head and looked at Father. Father was *crying!* Adam hadn't known he owned tears. This was the worst of all on this terrible day.

Father dropped to his knees and enfolded them into his arms, squeezing them tightly.

"I must keep you safe, my children. You cannot stay here where you might eat from the tree of life and live forever in your rebellion. Look! The door is opening!" Father's long arm was extended, finger pointing.

Adam and Eve stood and faced west. A massive door had indeed opened, and a stream of animals already made their way toward it. Adam took Eve's hand and pulled her away from the only home they'd ever known. As they reached the shimmering door into the unknown, they looked back and saw Father, still kneeling, still weeping.

They set their faces to the door and stumbled through. As soon as they did, the door blinked out with a mighty roar and disappeared. In its place a massive being stood, a flaming sword flashing back and forth as a warning.

Adam took Eve's hand, and they made their way into their new, silent world, their thoughts quieted within them, unable to hear each other unless they spoke out loud. Some of the small animals kept pace with them, but Adam saw some slink away with fear in their eyes.

How will we live without Father?

I am always with you, my son. Remember what I said. The serpent has the power to wound you, but the offspring of the woman will crush his head.

And Adam was comforted.

The man and woman were made for each other and for God. Perfect union, perfect communication, perfect surroundings. Nothing decayed, nothing died, no confusion, no misunderstandings. At the beginning, as the days melted into each other, Adam and Eve discovered each other and moved into ever-deepening intimacy with their Creator. You'd think it would be enough.

But it wasn't.

One day they encountered a creature who made them wonder what was missing in their lives. The creature created that wondering and then rushed to satisfy it. One moment they were completely content—and the next moment an unfamiliar longing for *more* played around the edges of their minds and tugged at their hearts. And that more destroyed them and the unique oneness they'd enjoyed with God. One moment they were innocent, living in perfect communion, and the next, mouths full of the forbidden fruit, they were guilty, unable to hear each other's thoughts, greed shrouding the Lover of their souls from view. Shut out from Eden, they trudged wearily away into an unfamiliar shadowed world with no plan, no peace, no future.

What was it they'd wanted? To *know*. To be like God. God had given them only one command—don't eat *that* fruit. They had every other tree, plant, and fruit at their disposal but this one. They had to have it—and the Lover of their souls took a backseat to their cravings.

And us...since they succumbed to the enemy, we have that same weakness in our DNA. More, must have more. We see...we want. We smell...we eat. We listen...we nod our heads in agreement. Yes, if we just had *that*, life would be perfect.

To what snake in the grass do you listen today? What forbidden fruit hangs in front of you right now? What shortcuts are you considering? What discontent blackens your heart, rudely shouldering the Lover of your soul to the sidelines of your mind?

Run! Back to Father, back to the safety of obedience, back to the shelter of contentment in Christ. That snake has no power to overtake you if you choose righteousness. Determine to be content with God's provision for you, disdaining the cheap baubles offered by this world. God desires so much more for you.

Choose to pause in your reach. Reconsider. Think. See eternally. And then watch that snake slither away.

For what do you reach today that God has not given you, shoving all other concerns aside?

Will you lay it down at his feet, content to own only that which comes from his hand?

Chapter 2
Offering

For they follow in the footsteps of Cain, who killed his brother.
~Jude 11

"Brother!" Cain called. "Where are you?"

He'd crashed through the brush, not bothering with stealth. In the midafternoon sun, the clearing was full of shadows. He heard the rustling of birds in the trees and the scamper of tiny feet—probably mice and rabbits—behind the foliage. He thought about snaring a rabbit or two, but discarded the idea. He was after bigger game—not the least of which was his errant brother.

He stood still, listening. It was always games with Abel, his junior by just hours. Cain thought perhaps it was due to his parents' surprise that there were two in her womb—and how long Abel had taken to present himself to them at birth. Perhaps he'd been playing games even then.

He cocked his ear at the sound of a faint snicker behind a thicket, and tiptoed over, suddenly throwing himself full length into the hedge. He landed squarely on...a family of deer resting there. They leaped up and ran, the female turning a baleful eye on him as if to scold his human antics.

Cain came barreling out of the thicket just in time to see his brother jump out on the opposite side of the small clearing, clutching his sides and laughing. Abel fell to his knees, gasping great draughts of air.

"Oh, brother, how funny you looked, leaping on those poor deer. I'll warrant you'd better stay out of that mother's way for a long time to come, lest she pummel you with her hooves."

Cain reached down and hauled the younger boy to his feet.

"Enough of that! Stop being silly. We have work to do, and it's not getting done. Our father will surely punish us if we come home with nothing."

"All right, all right. Where do we go from here?" Abel always deferred to his brother's superior hunting skills.

"This way. See if you can keep up."

The two brothers set off into the wooded area south of the small camp where their parents awaited their coming. Mother would already have the fire stoked and ready for meat, and Father would be tending Abel's small flock of goats and lambs in his absence. He hoped Father would also pick the grain to be used in tonight's supper and save him the trouble when they returned.

Much later, later than Cain had intended, they trudged home with a gazelle shouldered between them. They'd had to wait a long time, hidden in the rocks, for their prey to come close enough. But patience won out, and Cain's arrow had flown straight and true and brought him down with only one shot to the neck. It would make good eating for this night and the next several nights.

As they broke through the trees into the camp, Mother looked up and saw them, then put two fingers in her mouth and whistled. Father came running from the field behind their shelter, a basket of grain bouncing with each step. His eyes lit up when he saw the gazelle's carcass.

"Oh, well done, boys!" He set the basket down near Mother and knelt to inspect their catch.

"One shot, Cain? Only one?" he asked admiringly.

"Yes, Father, only one."

"Let me see your quiver."

Cain unstrapped the leather pouch from his back and handed it over. Adam removed an arrow, put it to his eye, and peered down the length of it. He rolled the shaft between his fingers, twisting it over and over. Cain waited for his father's comment. He glanced at Abel, who'd moved over by Mother and was obviously bored by their conversation.

"My son, how did you make this arrow so smooth? There is not one flaw in the wood that I can feel." He peered down the length of it again. "And so straight! What is your secret?"

"Ah, Father, shall I give away my secret for nothing?" Cain joked.

Adam laughed with him, then turned to Eve.

"This son of ours is a talented boy, my love."

"Yes, he is," she replied, a loving arm around Abel. "They are both gifts from the One."

The family busied themselves stripping and cleaning the carcass. They placed it on the fire to roast along with the grain. The conversation was low and pleasant and peppered with love and laughter.

***

Adam, much later—in the dead of night—awoke to that voice he knew, had known in the garden of God. He didn't often hear it audibly anymore. More often it was a thought or a suggestion drifting across his consciousness that he knew came from the Creator.

"Yes? I am here, Father," Adam said once out of earshot of the others. He followed the path to Cain's grain fields and stopped there, not wishing to wake the rest of the family.

"Adam, my son, I have instructions for you. You must teach this to Eve and to your two sons. I am Creator God, and you must learn how to worship me, that your hearts will always be pure and attuned to me. Are you ready to listen?"

"Yes, Father, I am ready," Adam said, and he knelt there among the ripe heads. He marveled that even the shafts of grain swayed and bowed as if also worshiping the Creator who made them grow.

As Father spoke, Adam closed his eyes and reveled in the closeness he had once enjoyed with Adonai in the garden. The moon climbed high in the sky as Father explained the requirements for proper worship of him. He made sure Adam understood each command and made him repeat back what he spoke.

At one point in the lesson, when Adam concentrated particularly hard, he opened his eyes and could have sworn he saw a tall shadow just a few paces away. He squinted. Yes, it was Father, and the joy Adam felt in that moment, after such a long time, was unbounded and threatened to put him on his face.

"Yes, my son, I am here with you and have made myself visible for just this little while. I told you when you left my garden I would never leave you."

"Thank you, Father, for allowing me to see you with my eyes, however dim and short the time." Adam reached out, and the shadow moved closer, mingling with him for just a moment. Adam was flooded with peace and confidence.

Oh, it has been so long…

"My son, my physical form will leave you now, but my Spirit is always with you. Make sure you share what I have told you with the woman and with *both* of your sons."

"Yes, I promise, Adonai. I will make sure they understand so that they, too, will worship you properly and will enjoy this closeness with you." He stood then and hesitated, gazing across the fields Cain tended with such diligence.

"You have a question."

"Yes, Father. How long will it be?"

"Many times must pass before we live together again. Evil must be conquered."

Adam felt sad at that, for he knew that evil would not need conquering but for his and Eve's rebellion. He willingly shouldered the blame for that. Adonai had first told him about the tree, and he should have stopped Eve from succumbing to its

allure. He felt a large hand on his shoulder, although he could not see it.

"My son, Adam, you are an honorable man. The many times will pass, and we will live together again. That is my promise to you this night. Make sure you teach these things to your wife and sons."

The shadow then faded away, leaving Adam alone again, but with such a glad comfort in his heart that he lay down right where he was and fell into a deep, dreamless sleep.

Eve found him there at dawn, and he told her everything Father had said. Her wonder matched his own. They covenanted together that their boys and any children who might come after would know and love Adonai, learn his ways, and obey his commands.

***

Many years passed. Cain and Abel grew to young manhood, taught by their parents to love God. Adam had taught himself how to make tools, which he in turn taught his sons. They experimented with ways to grow new plants, and with methods to get water to the crops, and how to harness certain animals to help with the harvest.

Eve practiced new ways of cooking the food the men brought to her. She found that some seeds and berries, when mixed together, yielded a delicious flavor when added to meats and grains. Day followed peaceful day as the little family worked together. Nights were spent worshiping Father, talking about him, sharing stories. The parents delighted in telling their sons tales of their life in God's garden before their children had been born. They told and retold the story of how Father had made Eve, and the sons never tired of hearing it.

One evening in particular, the two young men had a question. They'd finished supper and were reclining on animal skins around the waning firelight. The boys lay close together, whispering an argument.

"You ask them—you're the one who brought it up to me," Cain said.

"You're older. You should ask."

"All right, boys," Adam interrupted. "Ask what?"

Abel and Cain sat up. Cain stared at his brother, waiting. Finally, he shrugged and plunged in. "Father, God gave Mother to you. What about us? Will he give us wives? And who will they be—there is no one here except us four."

Adam glanced at Eve. With an amused smile, she gestured to him that the question was all his to answer.

"Well, hmm, I'm sure he will, Cain. Father has his own timing for things, and sometimes we really don't know what he's planning until we're staring at it."

He shot a look at Eve, and she broke into peals of tinkling laughter. Soon they were both laughing—that was, until Adam noticed the twin exasperation on his sons' faces. He touched Eve's arm, and they stopped immediately. Eve busied herself with some mending, glancing at Adam through lowered lids.

"Umm, sorry, boys. I guess you'd have to have been there. I do remember Father laughing at me the same way we were just now. He said he wished I could see my own face when I saw your mother for the first time."

Cain and Abel looked at him without speaking.

"Anyway, enough of that. As I was saying, when the time is right, Father will attend to giving you both wives. Until then, you will just have to be patient. Understand?"

"Of course, Father." Abel always submitted first.

Cain usually had to think things through for a time. And this time was no different, for when Adam glanced his way, he was just disappearing along the path to his grain field. Adam's shoulders drooped.

I wish he would just accept things—it would be so much more pleasant.

He turned to see Abel watching him.

"Father, he'll be fine. You know how he is—always has to sort things out for himself. Why, just the other day, he was wondering

why animals have to be brought for worship. He said he had plenty of grain to spare and asked why he couldn't just bring some of that instead."

Adam looked worried.

Eve came to him and laid a hand on his arm. "Adam, you'd better remind him that worship of Father must be done in his way. We can't just make up our own rules." A shadow passed over her face as she said it.

"Eve, please don't fret. This is not the same thing as when—"

"Isn't it?" she interrupted, her brow furrowed.

"Same thing as what?" Abel asked. He looked from one to the other.

Neither answered him.

Adam turned away from her and gazed toward the field. He could just see Cain walking slowly, brushing the heads of grain with his hands.

"I'll talk to him. I'll talk to him tomorrow."

Eve turned and went into the shelter, and Adam disappeared through the trees, leaving Abel alone at the fire.

***

Sometime later, at the time of the harvest, Adam returned to their home with a ram he'd slain for the evening sacrifice. Abel had accompanied him and helped him choose the fattest and healthiest in the small herd. Adam knew Abel's affection for his animals and that this was especially hard for him. Cain already had the fire prepared and had laid his offering next to it.

Adam was surprised to see the folded cloth at Cain's feet. He looked carefully around and didn't see an animal.

"Cain, I thought you were hunting in the northern hills today—for a sacrifice. You said you would take your best bow and find the biggest deer for your offering. I don't see it. Were you not successful, my son?" Adam stepped closer and pointed at Cain's feet. "What is in the cloth?"

Cain didn't look at him. "My offering," he said flippantly.

"Do not speak to your father in that tone. Answer his question. And it's mine too, son. The cloth is too small and too clean to contain an animal sacrifice."

"Yes, brother, what is it? Are going to keep us in suspense?" Abel said smoothly, clearly trying to lessen the tension.

He flipped open the cloth with his toe and squatted down, putting his hand inside. "It's grain," he said, looking puzzled. "What kind of sacrifice is that? We talked about this."

"It's my kind of sacrifice. Why shouldn't God be pleased with the fruits of my labor? He made me a tender of crops, not a herder of animals. So why can't he be pleased with my offering? It's what I do best, isn't it?"

His challenging tone rankled Adam. He pushed Abel out of the way and faced his older son.

"It is not for us to choose how we worship the One. I thought I'd made clear to you the lesson he taught me…"

"How do we know the lesson, as you call it, came from him? Maybe it was just something you dreamed after eating a bad piece of meat that night."

Adam made the leap to his son's side in one step, cuffing him on the side of the head. Cain didn't move, just reached up and rubbed his face where his father's hand had connected.

The two men faced each other, the firelight flickering and lending its own heat to the already charged atmosphere. The grain offering lay between them. Cain was now at least half a head taller than Adam, well muscled, while Adam had developed signs of age. Still, Adam judged he could put his son on the ground if it came to it.

I breathed the air of God's garden, and it still circulates through my lungs. He has only the weak air of this dark world in his.

They took each other's measure, Cain also clearly sizing up his chances in a fight.

"How like men to reduce our worship time to a physical contest," Eve said, reaching down and picking up the grain offering at their feet. They were startled, not having seen her approach.

"Cain, my son, you must make your offering as God wishes. You can't thwart him. I know you have not seen the One as we have, so you must trust us on this." Her smooth words did much to release the tension between father and son. She held the cloth out to Cain, who took it with a snarl, clutching it to his breast.

Adam turned away from Cain then and bowed his face to the ground. Shoulders shaking, he lifted his voice aloud and pled for his son, that the One would forgive his rebellion and would help him see that he must obey. Eve and Abel joined him, their voices blending together as they prayed.

As Adam ended the prayer, he raised his head to see Cain standing in front of the fire with the grain cloth in his hands. He stared at his father, his face strained, sweat leaking in rivers and dripping off his chin. He raised the cloth high over his head, turned suddenly, and flung it into the fire. Eve started forward but was stayed by Adam's hand on her arm.

"My son, what have you done?" Adam cried. The memory of those words spoken to him by Father so many times ago assailed his senses.

Eve wept at his side, turning her face away. Abel stood in shock, unable to speak.

Adam and Cain watched the grain lay untouched in the fire, flames licking all around it. God's fire did not descend and consume it. It did not come.

Cain raised his hands to the dark, silent heavens and cried out to God. "The One—where are you? I have given you my best effort, and yet you are silent! Why must it be thus?"

The crackling fire was the only answer. Cain fell to his knees and wept. Eve went to him then, knelt beside him, her mother's heart clearly breaking for him. She cried with him, tried to take him into her arms as she'd done when he was young, but he angrily shook her off.

"Mother, please stop."

He stood then, faced his father and his brother, fists clenched tightly at his sides.

"Fine, you win. I guess it's Abel's turn to try to appease this capricious God we serve."

He stepped back, standing in the shadows, face set. Feet set wide apart and arms crossed against his chest, he waited for his challenge to be answered.

Abel glanced at his father. Adam nodded slightly. He leaned over and helped Eve to her feet and drew her away from the fire. Her face was grief ravaged, tears streaking down to her chin, following the age lines. They stood together, arms wrapped tightly around each other.

She put her lips to his ear and whispered. "How did our worship time become a contest, my love?"

Adam shook his head and squeezed her shoulders tightly against him.

"Perhaps the One will have mercy on him—I have prayed for it," Eve whispered sadly.

Mercy, Father. Please let it be as your daughter has prayed.

He turned slightly and saw that Abel had finally wrestled their offering to the fire and was preparing to heave it in. He was having trouble lifting the huge ram by himself. He turned to his brother in mute appeal for help. Cain didn't budge, clearly unwilling to relent from his rage long enough to lend a hand.

Adam left Eve and went to Abel's side. Together they raised the ram and threw it into the raging fire, then stepped back to watch. They had repeated this process every season since the One had spoken to Adam, and every season they had witnessed the same result. Tonight was no different.

As the ram was slowly consumed by the man-made fire, God-made fire descended from a tiny glowing door in the dark sky directly overhead—a huge ball of fire that shot down and instantly obliterated the ram, the wood, even the water standing ready nearby in reed jars. As soon as the offering was consumed, the fiery orb retreated the same way it had come, traveling up the lightning bolt and disappearing into the opening far overhead. At the last moment, the door in the sky closed with a loud clap of thunder, leaving the four humans again under a dark sky.

Perfectly visible atop the small mound of ash was Cain's grain cloth, untouched, without even a wisp of smoke curling above it.

No one moved for many moments. Adam dropped to his knees, then to his face, uttering loud praises to God. Eve and Abel followed suit, lying prostrate with faces buried in their hands.

***

Cain stood where he was. As he watched the other three, a glow suffused over them from above, dim golden light bathing them as they lay in the dirt. His father rolled over, seeing Cain watching. The golden light faded as Father stood and faced his son. Mother and Abel sat up and clutched each other, Mother's face buried in her son's neck.

"My son, you can stand in his presence?" Father asked softly.

"Whose presence, Father?" The question lay between them, unanswered.

Cain looked up into the dark sky, then back at his father. "You can spend your life groveling in the dirt if you want. Not me."

He turned and grabbed his bow and his arrow pouch and headed into the night.

***

Cain stayed away from home for many weeks. But one day he tired of no company, no brother to tease, and having to eat his own cooking.

He appeared silently at first light one fine morning to see his mother slicing roots into a new pot.

"Mother!"

His mother, clearly startled, looked up. She dropped the flint into the pot and ran to him. Cain grabbed her in a great bear hug as she cried against his chest.

"Oh, Cain, you're back! How I've missed you, my son!"

He swung her around and around until her shrieks of laughter brought Cain's father out of the shelter. He watched the spectacle for a moment, then whistled for Abel. Father slowly approached as Cain gently set his mother down on her feet. She clung to his arm, turning a pleading look on Adam.

The two men eyed each other, then fell into each other's arms.

"Oh, my son, you have returned to us. Your brother will be so pleased."

"And you, my father, are you pleased?"

"Yes, yes, of course I'm happy you're back. How can you even ask?"

Cain noted his father's eyes couldn't quite meet his own. He shrugged.

"Well, as you say, I'm back. And I'm famished, Mother. Cooking my own meals has been…well, shall we say 'inadequate' and leave it at that?" Cain leaned over the pot and sniffed.

"What do you have here, Mother? Do I smell rabbit stew?"

She nodded.

"It smells different though."

"Your father discovered something we call *ajwan* seed. I've been trying it out in several different dishes. What do you think?"

"It smells good, but I'll reserve judgment until I've tasted it." He noted her disappointed expression at his halfhearted enthusiasm.

"Mother, it already smells better than what I've endured these past weeks." He patted her shoulder.

"Brother!" Abel shouted as he ran down the path. He stumbled over a rock as he gained the clearing, landing in a heap in front of Cain. He groaned and rolled over.

Cain helped him up, dusting him off and punching him on the shoulder in the process.

"Ow! You pack quite a punch. Have you been practicing on bears?"

Cain laughed and turned aside for a moment to pick up a small knife Abel had dropped. He turned just in time to see Abel's rush, hands extended. Cain hastily stepped backward, only to encounter Abel's right foot placed strategically behind his ankle. He fell to his seat with a thud, Abel neatly plucking his knife out of Cain's hand as he went down. Both boys laughed uproariously, joined by Adam and Eve, looking on with obvious pride.

"Well, brother," Cain said, "and who have you been practicing on?"

"Father, of course. He's been teaching me how to fight, to protect myself."

Cain threw an inquisitive look at his father. "From whom does he need protection, Father?"

Silence followed Cain's question.

"Well, no matter." He shrugged and turned back to Abel, a good-natured grin splitting his face. "Now you have someone else to practice on. What do you say we go hunting after this meal. You can show me your moves."

Joy blew across Abel's face. He gripped Cain's hand. "It's good you're back. Now I have someone else to talk to. I've had to do with Mother and Father as my only conversation for too long."

"Boys, go wash..." Eve started.

"See what I mean, brother?"

They smirked at each other, and arm in arm they went down to the nearby creek to wash.

***

Day followed day as Cain settled back into the family routines. He spent much time putting his grain fields to rights after having been away for so long. He helped Mother with chores, sparred with Abel, and hunted for game.

He kept his distance from Adam, however. They often eyed each other warily, as if each was waiting for the other to either throw a punch or offer a hug.

Evening worship time was uncomfortable for Cain, and soon he was slipping out to the fields before it began, not returning until the fire had burned down to embers. He'd slink back to the family group, no one saying much to him—except Abel, who always tried to smooth over the mounting tension.

Things came to a head one evening, though, just as they arose from worship. Cain reappeared and helped himself to more supper, still simmering on the cook fire. Adam arose from his place next to Eve and approached Cain with obvious purpose.

"My son, where have you been?"

"Out."

Adam's fists tightened at his sides, forearm muscles bulging, feet wide apart in a challenging pose. Cain read the signs and planted one foot slightly in front of the other and reached back to finger his arrows strapped in the pouch between his shoulder blades. His other hand lay softly on the sheath strapped to his thigh.

"Out? That's your explanation? Your explanation for why you no longer worship our God with us?"

"Your God, Father, not mine. I thought I'd made that clear to you."

Cain turned at the audible intake of breath from Eve. She looked at him through frightened eyes. Abel had frozen in the act of picking up stray pieces of firewood. All eyes were on Cain.

There's no time like the present, he thought.

"I'm sorry, Mother," he said somewhat grudgingly, for he wasn't really sorry. "I no longer worship your God. I no longer worship any god. Why should I? I've never seen him, never heard his voice. All I have is your stories of him, which you can't verify. How do I know for sure that he is who you say he is?" He stopped, seeing his mother's broken heart etched on her lined face.

"Mother, I don't begrudge you your worship of him. Or yours, Father. I just can't bow down to this unseen deity who chooses one over another according to his own whims. Truly," he said more gently, "I have no wish to hurt you. I just want to be left alone to worship or not worship the way I see fit. Is that too much to ask?"

Eve rose, went to Cain, and laid her forehead on his chest. His arms went around her as she wept. She looked up at him, face shining wet in the moonlight.

"My son, you do not understand what you are doing. Rebelling against the very One who made you?" She glanced at

Adam, who stood with bowed head. "Cain, your father and I know exactly what you are doing, and we can attest to the outcome for you."

Cain pushed her away and said angrily, "Yes, yes, another of your stories. Where is this shining door that blinks out in a moment before your very eyes? Where is this angel with the fiery sword, guarding the way into the garden of God? Point to where it is, Mother, so I can go and find it."

She stood mutely before him.

"Yes, I thought not. You don't even know in which direction to point. I have searched the hills for this doorway, spent hours in places none of you have explored. It's either gone or never was. I'm through with your fantastical stories of the unseen one."

Adam came to life at Cain's tone. He rushed Cain, arms extended, fury on his face. Cain neatly sidestepped him and whipped around, placing his left hand on his father's neck and shoving. Adam's momentum carried him, stumbling, close to the still-hot embers of the cooking fire. He tripped over a piece of wood and fell headlong, one arm landing in the fire.

Shrieking in rage, Adam sprang to his feet and rotated to face Cain again, only to be met with Cain's right hand, extended and gripping his big killing knife—the one he used to gut animals. Adam froze.

Eve ran to Adam's side, crying out for both of them to stop. Abel turned and disappeared. Cain heard his brother's feet pounding through the brush.

Eve whimpered at Adam's side as she tried to inspect the burns on his arm. He shook her off and pushed her behind him as he faced Cain. They stared at each other for a long moment, neither of them moving. Finally Cain lowered his flint and replaced it in its sheath. Adam exhaled slowly. He reached behind him and found Eve's hand, stroking it gently. Then he clasped both hands in front of him, visibly relaxing his muscles.

"My son," he said gently, eyes locked on Cain's, "your mother's right. You don't know what you're playing at."

Cain shrugged. "Well, then it's my game, isn't it? Nothing for you to get all worked up about."

Adam shook his head.

"We love you, son. But we cannot have you here with us if you refuse to worship God."

"Adam!" Eve cried. "What are you saying?"

Cain stared at Adam with a measured look.

"He's telling me to leave, Mother. Isn't that right, Father?"

"I don't want it this way, son. But we can't have you here, tainting our worship and teaching Abel to doubt the existence of the One."

"He'll doubt of his own accord someday."

Eve stepped in front of Adam. "Cain, please listen to us. Please do not do this." She turned to Adam, gripping his hands in her own, face upturned. "Please, Adam, do not send him away. Perhaps under our guidance—"

Cain stopped her.

"No, Mother, your wishing will not make it so." He looked over her head at his father. "May I stay the night? I'll leave at first light."

"Yes. First light will be fine," Adam replied softly.

He extended his hand and Cain took it, gripping it hard.

"I'm sorry, Father. Sorry it came to this. But it must be this way."

Eve tore away from Adam and ran into the shelter, where they could hear her moaning in anguish. Adam turned and followed her without a backward glance.

Cain waited for Abel's return for a long while, then finally gave up and trudged out to sleep in the grain field.

***

Morning arrived with no sign of Abel. Cain gathered his arrows and the rest of his knives and left before his parents awakened. He headed in the direction Abel had fled hours ago, certain where he'd find him. Abel had proudly shown him the spot a short time ago. He called it his thinking place—a small opening in the dense trees about half a day's trek from home. Abel had cleared the brush away from a small depression in the ground and moved some rocks and small logs into a rough circle where he liked to sit. From that vantage point, he had said, he often saw deer and rabbits peering at him from the surrounding trees. Once, he'd said, a small deer had come right up to him and taken grass from his hand.

Cain remembered the story as he trudged the last bit of ground before clearing the rise near the spot. He remembered with shame his response to his brother's story and the stricken look Abel had turned on him. *Why didn't you grab the little creature and wring its neck? It would have made a tender supper for us.*

As he climbed to the top of the rise that overlooked the clearing, he heard a noise in the brush off to the right. He had an arrow strung on his bow before he saw that Abel watched the spot from below. Letting the arrow fly, he rushed down the small hill, another arrow already loaded.

"No!" Abel yelled. It was too late. The first arrow found its mark on the deer's neck, dropping it. Cain replaced the second arrow in the pouch and turned just before Abel's fist smashed into his face. Blood gushed from Cain's nose.

Falling backward, he tripped over a stump and rolled the rest of the way down the hill. Abel stumbled after him, jumping on top of him, pummeling him with his fists. Cain defended himself, putting up his arms to block the hardest blows, but otherwise he did not fight back. He could easily have subdued him, but Cain had no wish to hurt his brother.

Finally, Abel rolled off of him, lying on his back and gulping for air. Tears lay on his cheeks.

"His name was Ayyal," he said, sitting up and wiping off his cheeks. "I saw his mate the other day. She was large with young."

Cain was silent. He stared in the direction of the dead animal, trying to feel Abel's sorrow. He couldn't dredge it up.

"Why do you name the animals we must kill and eat?"

Abel shrugged. "It's what Father did at the beginning."

"So he says. Don't you ever wonder if their tales of before are strictly true?"

"No. Why would they lie?" Abel followed his brother's gaze to Ayyal. "I guess he must now be sacrificed to the One."

"It would make more sense to eat him, brother."

Abel, with a troubled look, ignored the suggestion.

"Will you help me get him home?"

Cain stood and stretched, extending a hand to Abel. They walked slowly to the animal's carcass.

"I'll help you prepare it. Then we'll carry it home—we should be able to handle it together. Do you have your knife?"

"Yes. Will you stay?" Abel asked.

"No. But perhaps after we get home with it, we can go to the fields before I leave."

They worked together, quickly dressing out the large deer and wrapping it in the hunting cloth Cain always carried with him.

Cain felt Abel's eyes on him as they finished. He could hardly wait to get this job done and be on his way.

He's my brother, but he's a stranger...like Father and Mother. Or perhaps I'm the stranger.

***

Cain and Abel reached the shelter late that evening after their parents were asleep. They left the deer near the waning fire and struck out for the grain fields to spend the night as they used to when young boys.

They lay down side by side, talking softly. Abel tried to convince Cain to return home and reconcile with Father. Finally Abel gave up and rolled over to sleep. Sometime in the night, the fury in Cain's heart overtook him. He arose silently, gazed at the sleeping form of his brother, but saw only one thing—his sack of grain resting untouched on the fire. His offering rejected by God. He'd told his parents that he'd never heard God speak, but that was a lie. He'd heard the voice that very night, the night Abel's sacrifice was accepted and his own rejected.

Leaving Your Lover

Why are you so angry? Why do you look so dejected? You will be accepted if you do what is right. But if you refuse to do what is right, then watch out! Sin is crouching at the door, eager to control you. But you must subdue it and be its master.

The words of the One now burned his brain, searing right down into his heart. He picked up a large rock and held it over his head. His muscles strained with the effort as he hesitated, his eyes searching the heavens.

Will you not stop me?

There was no answer. Cain brought the rock down on his brother's head, hearing the sickening crunch. He stood for a moment. Nothing changed. No thunderbolt from heaven, no voice, no heavenly army come to slay him for his sin.

Cain dug a small depression just outside the far border of his field, dragged his brother's body to it, and covered it over with rocks and brush. He sat next to the grave all night, waiting for God's retribution, but it never came. He lay down and slept.

The next morning he awakened early and went to the small lake on the other side of a small stand of trees near his field. He knelt to wash, saw his reflection in the clear water, and staggered back in shock. He put his hand to his forehead and traced the outline. He crept back to the water and looked again.

A mark was stamped on his forehead, a strange symbol looking like two rough tree limbs crossed. It glowed faintly reddish, outlined in black. Cain stared, trying to figure out the meaning.

"Cain, my son, where is your brother?"

Cain jumped to his feet, startled, turning round and round, searching for the owner of the voice.

"I don't know. Am I his guardian?"

"What have you done? I hear your brother's blood crying to me from the ground."

Cain dropped to his knees then, hands covering his face. Still, his heart would not yield.

"So be it. You are now cursed and banished from the ground, which has swallowed your brother's blood. You will no longer be able to wrest crops from the ground no matter how hard you work. From now on, you will be a homeless wanderer on the earth."

"My punishment is greater than I can bear. You have banished me from the land I love and from your presence. You have made me a homeless wanderer. What if someone kills me?"

"No, anyone who tries to kill you will receive a sevenfold punishment from me. The mark I placed on your forehead will cause others to fear you. And every time you look at it or touch it, you will remember your shame."

Cain bowed his head, knowing now—as the presence retreated and the voice quieted—that the One existed. His parents were right after all. He reached up and fingered the mark, shame flooding his soul.

Protected and judged.

Cain stood to his feet, settled the pouch at his back, and struck out to the other side of the lake, east toward the land his father had named Nod.

The sun had climbed a quarter of the way into the sky when he stopped to rest. He found a sheltered spot halfway up a smooth slope. He could still see the valley where lay his field and Abel's broken body. Coming up out of a small pool, he heard a faint sound from the west. Shaking the water out of his ears, he heard the keening wail as it rode on the wind. His parents had found his brother.

He turned and continued his journey east.

Cain couldn't find it within himself to follow God's rules for worship. His path led to hell as surely as rejection of Messiah in our day.

God gives us only this one rule for worship, spoken by Jesus in John 14:6: "I am the way, the truth, and the life. No one can come to the Father except through me."

We sugarcoat this command, not wanting to step on the toes of those who refuse to worship God altogether or who practice a faith that excludes Messiah Jesus. We shrink back from telling God's truth, unwilling to love others enough to tell them the path they're on leads away from the God they seek, away into an eternity as desolate as the scape of the farthest known planet.

Be assured, when we reach home, we will know—if only for an instant—who is not there because we were too timid in this world to lead them to the right path.

Will you follow this one rule—Jesus is the only route to God—and share it with others he places in your path?

What self-made rules for worship enslave you today? Will you choose to approach the living God through faith in Messiah?

How will you share with others whom God has placed in your path the one rule he has given us for worship?

Chapter 3
The Lie

At that time a severe famine struck the land of Canaan, forcing Abram to go down to Egypt, where he lived as a foreigner.
~Genesis 12:10

Abram shaded his eyes against the glaring desert sun. "We're here."

He looked west into the land of Egypt. After traveling over three hundred miles, they had finally reached their destination. He fell to his face, the entire company following suit. Clouds of dust and sand rose around them and covered them as they worshiped God.

"I Am, thank you for bringing us all this way." Abram's strong voice lifted above the throng. "Merciful God, keep us safe here, and may we do all you require us to do. May there be enough food for all of us, and may you cause the Egyptians to be generous. And please bring us back to the land of promise before too many days go by. All glory to the great I Am."

Rising, he dusted his robes and looked tenderly at Sarai as he helped her to her feet.

"Will we continue on today, Abram? The children are weary. Perhaps we should stop here for the night and move on in the morning, when it's cooler."

Abram considered her words. It was well past midday, and the sun would soon set. It wouldn't hurt to let the company rest here—then in the morning, it would be an easy walk into Egypt. He judged it would take no more than a half day. He searched the landscape just south of their position and saw the green of a small oasis. Nodding his head, he placed his hand on her shoulder.

"Just a bit farther, Sarai. Look yonder," he said, pointing. "Do you see that shimmer? We'll walk only to that point and rest. There'll be shade there, and we can cook a real meal."

He struck out, leading his people to the oasis. Behind him he could hear the cheerful voices of women and children, excited that the push to escape the famine in Canaan was almost over.

Sarai had dropped behind him to walk with the other women. He glanced behind him and saw her scoop a small child into her arms, her infectious laughter tinkling over the sand. The prayer on his heart winged its way to the I Am once again—the same prayer planted in his heart ever since the day God blessed him and promised to make a great nation out of him. Smiling, he remembered Sarai's reaction when he told her of the stupendous promise.

"A great nation from you, Abram?" she'd asked, her dark eyes round like an owl's. "A nation? All I want is one child. Did you ask him about that?"

Sarai always spoke her mind, and it was what he loved about her. He'd shushed her and told her to have faith. The day would come. God always kept his promises.

As he walked and prayed, the murmur of voices behind him a soothing backdrop, he marveled that none had been lost on this journey. Surely God was with them, guiding them. The burden of leading God's people felt a little lighter with each step, his sturdy staff punching the hot sand at intervals. The I AM had promised to guide, and he had. He'd promised to provide, and he had. He'd promised to keep them safe, and he had. Gratitude bloomed in Abram's heart. Nothing could possibly go wrong as long as he kept to the path of faith in God.

They reached the oasis and set up camp in the shade of a few straggly thorn trees. In the sand was a deep depression with water. The women quickly filled jars and their children's mouths. After they'd had their fill, the men led the camels to the water, the beasts noisily gulping and spitting.

They sat down in family groups and opened their packs of food, mostly dried figs and hard bread. Abram walked among the people, inspecting their stores. They were severely depleted. They'd reached Egypt just in time.

He made his way back to Sarai, who was with her friend, Abigail. Abigail and Nathan had seven children. Sarai was helping her corral the youngsters on the rough blanket she'd spread out for them to sit on. As he stood and watched, Sarai finally herded them to the blanket and sat them down in a semicircle. Abigail doled out the food, and the children ate greedily.

Father, she will make a wonderful mother. Thank you for your promise.

He beckoned to her, and she rose immediately, waving to Abigail. They strolled to the other side of the camp, where Sarai had already laid out their food. They sat close together as they ate, enjoying each other's company as they oversaw their people.

"Looks like the children are getting sleepy, husband," Sarai observed.

"Yes, they're tired. As I'm sure you are, my love. Why don't you stretch out right here and try to close your eyes. There's nothing that needs your attention at the moment, and I won't disturb you."

"Yes, I think I will."

She leaned back on the blanket and rolled to her side, pillowing her head in the crook of her elbow. It wasn't long before she fell asleep. Abram stood and gazed out over the company. Parents settled their children down for much-needed naps, some of them lying with their little ones.

He walked slowly down to the water and knelt to drink. He was joined by Nathan. He sank to his knees next to Abram and put his head under the water, coming up and shaking it out of his hair and beard.

"It's good to see everyone resting, isn't it?" Nathan asked, wiping water from his eyes and standing to his feet next to Abram. "Our youngest finally settled and is sleeping, as is Abigail. She needed it. Our brood is quite a handful."

"Yes, my friend, it is good that everyone is sleeping. Sarai is resting also."

"She's a good woman." He rested his hand on Abram's shoulder. "She will make a good mother."

"Ha! That's just what I told God today. I'm sure he agrees," Abram said with a small smile. "It was her idea, not mine, to go no further today."

"Then she's a wise woman also." He rubbed his eyes and his temples. "I think I'll go keep Abigail company. Maybe I can get a little sleep too. Will you wake me later to help you keep watch?"

Abram nodded.

The two men parted, Abram making his way back to Sarai's side. He sat down next to her, taking care not to wake her. His eyes traveled over her petite form, settling on her face—in repose, breathtakingly beautiful. Tendrils of her luxuriant black hair had escaped from their bonds and lay across the curve of her cheek. It was a wonder to Abram how she managed to look so stunningly alluring after walking the hot desert for days and days.

Abram leaned back on his elbows, stretching out his tired legs. His tunic was filthy. He looked forward to a proper bath when they reached an Egyptian settlement. He closed his eyes and lay down on his back, arms over his eyes against the last light from the setting sun.

A small worry burrowed itself into his mind, like an insect in a fruit. It had begun earlier today, when he'd first set his eyes on their destination in the distance. Just a hint of an impending...*something*. He'd ignored it then, but now he couldn't.

Egypt.

I might have standing with God's people, but here I'm an alien, a foreigner.

Leaving Your Lover

What would happen to them here? As far as Abram knew, there were no Egyptians who cared for God, sought his blessing, or followed his commands. How would his people be treated? He'd trusted God as they'd traveled here, but now they were here and he was suddenly unsure.

Perhaps it's because I made the decision to come. But what else could we do?

He opened his eyes. The sun had disappeared, and a cool breeze blew across the sand. It would be completely dark soon. He saw small pinpricks of light uncovered overhead. He turned his head and gazed at Sarai again, wanting to talk to her; she always helped him see the other side of things. She had the gift of being able to allay his fears with her calm assessment of any situation. Even as children, she'd always helped him see the bright side, her infectious cheerfulness making light of impending doom.

He leaned over to touch her shoulder, but stopped himself— no, he wouldn't wake her. She needed to rest.

As he watched Sarai sleep, the worry ballooned in his mind. How would he keep her safe? She was counted a beautiful woman in any culture. Would she be in danger? It was all well and good that they'd find food, but what would they be required to trade for it? They had some gold with them, but would it be enough? They were light on weapons, needing to pack food and supplies for the children, so they'd left their heavy weapons behind. Had that been a mistake? The insect of anxiety in his mind turned this way and that, chewing on his hitherto unshakeable faith in God.

I must make a backup plan in case things fall apart.

Abram leaned back again and dozed fitfully under the shining canopy, one arm draped over Sarai's shoulder. He felt the gnawing of the insect as he rejected one plan after another. Somewhere in the dead of the desert night, Abram decided what he must do.

***

"What?" Sarai asked incredulously, her face the color of the red cactus in bloom. "You're not serious, husband—you can't be!"

"Just hear me out, Sarai. You're a beautiful, desirable woman. We don't know what kind of man this pharaoh is."

"Abram, I won't do it!"

"Keep your voice down," he commanded her, looking over his shoulder to see if anyone was listening. "You're overreacting. You *are* my sister in truth."

"Oh, so I'm your wife when you need me but your sister when it suits you. I see."

Abram frowned in frustration. This was not going as he'd intended. He'd discounted Sarai's inborn stubbornness—it far outmatched his own.

"Sarai, we won't be here long. And I promise you, one look at you and my life will be only worth so much camel dung! But if we say you're my sister..." He trailed off, seeing the fleeting look of fear drift across her face. He judged she was close to capitulating and more words would be useless. He turned away from her, shoulders drooping. He waited, fully expecting another tirade. His plan would be useless unless she agreed. The tense moments fled by, husband and wife unyielding.

He was on the point of telling her to just forget the whole thing, when he felt her small hand in his. He turned swiftly to her, gathering her into his arms.

"Sarai, God will protect us. If we say you're my sister, I'll be treated well."

"If he can protect us, then why do we have to help him, husband? Can he not protect us without our help?"

"Of course he can. But—" He stopped, defeated by her logic, as always.

"But we have to make sure he will, is that it?" She looked down at her feet, a mere five feet from her head. She looked up again, eyes pressing into his.

"Have you considered what might happen to me while you're being 'treated well'?"

"Nothing will happen, my love."

Sarai shaded her eyes and looked west. Her face relaxed, the corners of her mouth lifting in the barest of smiles. Abram knew he'd won.

"You'll see. We'll stay here until the famine is gone. Then we'll go back home. I promise. Now I must see that everyone is ready to go."

He escaped her presence, turning only once to glance at her. He was relieved to see she'd begun to pack up their belongings for the trek to the nearest Egyptian settlement.

***

Hours later Abram knew he'd made the biggest mistake of his life. After standing in the hot sun awaiting the arrival of the pharaoh and his advisers, they'd finally been given permission to set up their camp on the far side of the city. They'd been given food and water. It looked like all would be well.

Then the pharaoh's advisers had come back with armed soldiers and had gathered up the women who'd taken their fancy. They took twenty-three of the most beautiful girls and several older women, including his beloved Sarai. They left some of those who had children, including Abigail.

"Call it payment for our hospitality," their commander had said, grasping Sarai's small frame by the shoulder. Her look of fear overwhelmed Abram. She was mute, shaking like a leaf in the wind. The commander was a behemoth next to her. He turned and walked away with her stumbling along next to him.

"Wait!" Abram called desperately. "May I at least say goodbye to my sister?"

The commander shrugged his shoulders and released her. She ran swiftly back to Abram and clutched his tunic.

"Abram—"

"No, Sarai, be careful what you say." He looked over her head at the watching commander. "I promise I will get you out. Just be calm and do as you're told. Don't fight, please, my wife. I will pray to God, and he will rescue you."

Her eyes narrowed as they searched his face.

"I shouldn't have to be rescued," she said bitterly. "But I will do as you say. See that you do what *you* have said."

The commander stepped to Sarai's side and grasped her elbow, turning her around to march her to the waiting camel. He threw a backward glance at Abram, indecision written across his face. He looked around carefully. There was no one near. The other soldiers had mounted their beasts with captives in tow.

He stepped closer. "Look—the pharaoh himself is interested in your sister. He will take her into his *harim*."

Abram's alarm must have shown on his weathered face, as the commander came even closer after checking again that the other soldiers were out of earshot.

"It's not as bad as you think, sir," the commander said kindly. "He won't touch her for at least a year. She must go through our ritual purification rites before he beds her. She will be quite safe and well cared for as long as she remains in the charge of the eunuchs. The pharaoh would instantly execute anyone who threatens her or lays a hand on her."

The commander stepped closer yet, within a foot of Abram.

"The stories of your God have reached us," he whispered. "Perhaps…perhaps he will rescue your *sister*."

Did he know?

Abram was silent, praying to God it would be as the commander described and that Sarai would be safe.

"Now go back to your encampment," the commander suddenly barked, all soldier again. "And see that you keep your people in line and out of trouble, or it will go hard for you—and for your sister. Pharaoh's patience with freeloaders wears thin."

"Yes. I will. And thank you, sir," Abram said softly.

The commander put Sarai on the kneeling camel and climbed up behind her, raising the camel to its feet with a jerk on the leather strap.

"Not a word of this conversation," he warned as he turned the camel.

Sarai threw a backward glance at her brother-husband. Her face was set, but now a calmness had also settled there. Abram knew she was praying, as he was.

The sound of weeping throughout the camp that night layered guilt upon guilt on Abram. He lay lonely in his tent, surrounded by his people, who now only scowled at him. How had he let this calamity befall them? He wrestled on his blanket, with himself, with God, with his tortured thoughts.

This is my fault. If only I'd made sure this is truly what God intended me to do to save this people—before we left. Perhaps he would have directed my steps in a different direction.

Abram's thoughts were interrupted by the sound of a scuffle outside his tent. He quickly got to his feet and approached the opening cautiously. Peering out, he saw Nathan subduing another man—a sheepherder named Baram. The moon shone brightly on them, and he could see a small crowd gathering in a ring around the men. He stepped out, pushing through the onlookers.

Nathan finally wrestled Baram to the ground—straddling him—both hands wrapped around his throat and his left knee pressing Baram's right shoulder into the sand. Abram saw the gleam of a knife in Baram's hand. As Nathan pressed harder on his shoulder, Baram finally let the blade drop with a moan. Abram bent swiftly and picked it up. Nathan stood and hauled Baram to his feet.

"This man was hiding behind your tent, Abram. I caught him sneaking around to the opening."

Abram looked from one to the other, then down at the shining blade.

"And what were *you* doing out here at this time of night, my friend?" he asked Nathan.

Nathan dropped his eyes to his feet and said nothing.

"Well? Will you answer me? It seems you both have some explaining to do."

Abram heard murmurs among the growing throng around them.

"Silence! Please."

They obeyed him as always, but he felt their eyes like needles piercing his flesh.

Nathan finally looked up and locked eyes with Abram.

"What was I doing? I was keeping you from being murdered in your sleep—that's what! Abram, do you know what these, your people, are thinking right now? Have you considered, after what has happened today, that your life is in danger? No, you lay in your tent, alone in your own sorrow—uncaring that you are the leader of this people. God has placed you here. You must address their fears, not hide in your tent pining for your wife. These men have lost their wives and sisters and daughters too. What will you do?"

The silent night breeze lifted his hair gently and swirled the sand at his feet. Abram's heart broke at his friend's words. Nathan stood in front of him giving him God's message. He looked up into the stars. His heart and mind shifted.

"You're right, my friend," he said softly and clasped Nathan's hand in a strong grip. "He's right!" he called loudly over the company. "We must pray together for the safety of our women."

Abram fell to his knees, then to his face, all the people following suit. He begged God and his people for forgiveness. They pleaded with God for the safe return of their women, their voices blending together in a song that reached beyond the sky.

The stories of Abram's God *were* true, as the commander and all of Pharaoh's household would discover. Just as Abram had told Sarai, he was treated like royalty because of her, while she languished in the care of Pharaoh's *harim*. Abram prayed for her rescue each day, but when it came, it was unlike anything for which he'd prayed—angels to surround the Egyptians, warriors

to ride from the heavens on the wind, or something as simple as an earthquake. God didn't send angelic help, or warriors from heaven, or an earthquake. God did something much more stunning—he spoke to Pharaoh directly, to a man who did not even believe Abram's God existed.

After enduring terrible plagues, God revealed to Pharaoh the true relationship between Abram and Sarai. Pharaoh lost no time in ousting Sarai from his household and evicting God's people. He may have been a tyrant, but he evidently balked at taking another man's wife. God put the fear of God into him.

Abram didn't doubt God's *ability* to protect Sarai—just his *will* to protect her, and went with his own plan to keep her safe. He fell flat on his face. We shake our heads in disbelief, don't we? How could Abram, who'd already seen with his own eyes God's provision, *not* trust him now?

But wait! When was the last time you and I were given a promise by God and then when things got scary, we promptly forgot it?

> Here on earth you will have many trials and sorrows. But take heart, because I have overcome the world. (John 16:33)

> I will always be with you; I will never abandon you. (Joshua 1:5)

Oh, blessed promise! We move out in the direction God has called us to go, but then we hit the long trek through the desert of this world—a famine of politics, troubling social issues, wayward children—and the fretting begins. We manipulate our loved ones to make sure *they* make the right choices, and we fret during sleepless nights about circumstances over which we have no control. I know—I've been there. I can't remember all the nights I've lain awake, worrying about my children and grandchildren, my parents, my own shortcomings, unwilling to let God wrest the trouble from my heart.

We're all Abrams. We receive with gladness God's sure promises, then become master schemers to make sure his plans come to pass.

Thank goodness God is still God and he didn't leave Abram going in that direction. He kept his promise. And thank goodness he watches my back, too, reminding me he has a plan for me and all those I love, and *he* will bring those plans to pass.

No need to know anything else.

Think About It...

Are you a schemer? Do you trust God's ability and will to protect and to guide you, or are you plagued by a sharp edge of doubt?

Will you lay down your fretting and let God be God?

Chapter 4
For a Mess of Pottage

So Esau swore an oath, thereby selling all his rights as the firstborn to his brother, Jacob.
~Genesis 25:33

He was almost home, and he was ravenous. The hunt had been wretched. He'd roamed the hill country for days but found nothing. Not even a rabbit had run across his path, nor a fox out of its den. The deer were shy this time of year, watching him from the shelter of the rushes near the water. He had nothing to offer his father, which brought sadness to his mind.

The old man surely can't live much longer. I must do my best to keep him comfortable and happy for the rest of his days.

As he stumbled, exhausted, over the last hillock and looked down into the valley toward home, he fancied he smelled something. Approaching, he was sure of it. The fragrance of lentil stew, his favorite, wafted on the soft evening breeze. He visualized his mother standing over the fire, stirring the pot as she awaited his coming.

Esau stepped around the tent, expecting to see Rebekah at the fire, but instead he saw Jacob.

Even better. His stew is better than Mother's. I wonder what his secret is.

Esau hurried back around to the front side of the tent and entered. Stripping off his outer clothing, he washed his hands and body quickly and put on a fresh tunic. He could hear Jacob humming softly as he worked. His gentle brother aggravated him sometimes—actually many times—the way he fawned over their mother, always looking for ways to please her with his reading of scrolls, his culinary talent, staying by her side most days. Esau preferred the wild countryside, the hunt, the kill. If he was honest with himself, as he always tried to be, he preferred his father's company to his mother's. He honored her as was her due, but didn't like to spend much time with her.

His father enjoyed the game Esau brought home and the way Esau cooked it. And that was good—very good—because some day, soon he hoped, he would inherit all of this. Esau wanted that inheritance, and as the firstborn of his father and mother, he was entitled to it—the double portion.

And so I must continue to please him. He is the only one who can confer upon me his land and his blessing. Jacob can have Mother's preference and affection. I want Father's possessions. *I've always been the practical son—Jacob's the dreamer.*

"Brother!" he called, coming around the tent and facing Jacob.

Jacob looked up, a faraway look in his eyes.

"Esau, you're back. You were gone a long time. How was the hunt?"

"Miserable, my brother, miserable. I saw nothing but spiders and beetles—nothing else moved out there."

Esau walked closer, lowering his head over Jacob's stew and watching him warily under his lashes. He was always gratified to see how his own bulk dwarfed his twin. Jacob was of slim build and gentle expression. His hands were delicate, like their mother's. He'd learned to fight alongside Esau, under their father's tutelage, and could usually hold his own against him— by stealth and deception rather than by brawn and muscle—but he'd be useless in a real fight. Esau knew Jacob was no match for Esau's own fighting skills, learned on the hunt, facing down lions and wild dogs and the occasional human looking for a scrap.

Jacob's gentle nature alone will probably get him killed one day.

He turned his attention back to the stew, his stomach rumbling.

"But what have we here? One of your concoctions, I'll wager. It smells good—and I'm hungry. Is it ready to eat?"

Jacob didn't answer. He continued to stir slowly.

"Brother? I asked you if it's ready to eat."

Still no answer.

Seriously aggravated now, Esau reached over the pot and grabbed his twin by the shoulder, giving it a shake.

"Will you ignore your elder, Jacob? I'm hungry and I want something to eat!"

Jacob looked up, his eyes narrowed as he raked Esau with his stare. Esau spared a moment to wonder what Jacob was thinking.

Probably no good for me. He's such a calculating, devious man, this brother of mine. I always have to watch my back around him.

"My brother, of course you can have some of this—your favorite," Jacob said smoothly, still watching Esau's face. "But it's not quite ready. The meat isn't completely cooked, and I have some spices here I need to add. Why don't you go in and visit with Father while I finish it."

Jacob's sideways glance at him through narrowed slits pricked his curiosity. *What is he up to now?*

Esau stepped into the tent and found his mother sitting on a low stool with some mending. She looked up at him, her lined face still beautiful.

"My son, I didn't see you come in. Your father's been awaiting your coming. You should go to him now."

Esau nodded and gave her an affectionate kiss on the cheek.

"Since Jacob's not gotten supper ready yet, I'll do that. That boy's lazy, Mother. You should be harder on him. Here I had a dismal hunt, and Father's probably hungry. It's long past time to eat. He'll be grumbling."

"Now, Esau, you mind your manners. Don't forget to whom you speak."

Esau shook his head but knew he shouldn't press her anymore. Father wouldn't like it if he found Esau had been pushing her. And above all, he must keep Father happy. It surely wouldn't be long now.

"All right, Mother, I'll go to him now. I'm sorry if I upset you."

She didn't look up. "Just go, my son," she said quietly.

He stood watching her a moment longer, wishing she'd at least smile at him. She reserved her motherly laughter and affection for Jacob—his twin was her favorite—but just a smile sometimes would be nice. Or an encouraging word.

A memory flashed through his mind while he stood over her. He and Jacob had been about five and they'd wandered too far from camp and become lost. They'd been out in the rough hills for half a day before they'd found their way back. Isaac had sent men out to look, but they'd been unable to find them. Esau had finally found the path they'd taken and dragged Jacob along with him. Jacob had been trying—he had wailed, resisted Esau's efforts to help him, and fallen several times, deep scratches marring his spindly little legs.

When they'd finally stumbled back into camp, their mother had gone to her knees before Jacob and clutched him to her breast, weeping over his safe return. Then she'd turned a baleful eye upon Esau and scolded him for allowing her precious boy to get lost and then to hurt himself.

Esau's face now flamed at the memory—she'd not spared even a question as to how he'd fared during the ordeal. All her concern was for delicate little Jacob. And she'd not thanked Esau for getting her favorite boy back to her. He'd run out to the fields to find Father, who'd clapped him on the shoulder in welcome.

At least Father had acted like he was glad to see me.

Rebekah looked up at him, lips set in a straight line.

"Well? Is there something else?"

Esau turned his back on her without answering and ducked into the inner chamber of the large tent. His father lay on cushions, snoring loudly, his head and shoulders propped up. Looking from the doorway, Esau was struck by how old he looked in the dim light. His head had fallen sideways, and his mouth was slimy with drool. His blind eyes were pinched shut. His chest rattled with each labored breath.

No, it won't be long.

He wished he could feel sadness over Isaac, at the very least for his mother, but he didn't. He'd always felt boxed in by his father's strict upbringing, and he longed to be on his own, the head of the family, caring for them as he knew he could, as he was born to do. After all, he was the eldest. He would never pretend to be sad, even for his mother's sake, so Esau didn't look forward to the days of mourning. But afterward…he would be calling the shots for the family dynasty his father and grandfather, Abraham, had built.

Esau sat cross-legged on the mat next to his father's bed. He laid a hand on Isaac's arm, causing the old man to stir, a fresh fit of coughing bringing him completely awake. The stench of Isaac's breath was nauseating, and the room smelled as if it hadn't been opened and aired for days.

"Who is that? Are you Esau?" Isaac asked, rasping out the words.

"Yes, it is I, Father—Esau, your firstborn," Esau answered.

Isaac let his hands travel up and down his son's arms, then leaned closer to him and sniffed.

"Yes, it is you. How was your hunt?"

"It was miserable, Father. But I'll go out again tomorrow."

"Yes, yes. Go again tomorrow, and God be with you. But what am I to eat? I'm hungry, wasting away here on this bed."

"My husband," Rebekah said from the doorway, "Jacob has cooked a savory lentil and goat-meat stew for you. Isn't he a good boy? He will bring you some in just a little while."

Isaac grunted disagreeably. "Yes, I suppose he's a good boy. Too slim and weak for my tastes though. Now Esau, just look at how well muscled and strong he is. I wish these old eyes could see him. He's a man—and a superb hunter. I like the way he cooks my meat."

Rebekah came swiftly to Isaac's side and knelt, putting her head on his breast.

"Both of our sons have God's gifts, Isaac. Esau is a strong man, a leader, and as you say, a skilled hunter. But Jacob has his talents—he's a thinker, a planner. Isn't that important too?"

Isaac patted his wife's luxuriant hair, running his hand down the full length of it to the small of her back. She nestled deeper into the crook of his shoulder.

"Yes, Rebekah, they both have gifts. And I thank God for both of them every day I draw breath."

Rebekah grasped him tighter, closing her eyes. Isaac's head dropped back to the cushions again. The tick of a beetle was the only sound that could be heard.

Esau, now feeling like an intruder, got up quietly and backed to the doorway, leaving his parents to this fleeting moment of intimacy. He was now seriously hungry.

"Jacob," he called from the entrance to the tent, "is it ready now? Our father needs to eat, and so do I."

As Esau approached the fire, Jacob ladled the stew into a large bowl that Esau had claimed for his own. He was careful to pick out big chunks of goat meat. He did it slowly, carefully arranging each spoonful in the bowl.

Esau's mouth hung slightly open, watching each heaping mound of stew dropped into the bowl. Fidgeting, he drew the back of his hand across his mouth.

"Will you hurry up, brother? This isn't a piece of artwork here—it's my dinner! I just want to eat it." He reached for the bowl.

Jacob moved it slightly out of his reach.

"Come on, Jacob—quit teasing!"

Jacob placed the ladle to the side of the iron cooking pot, holding the bowl closely in front of him.

Leaving Your Lover

"Esau, I've been thinking. You look hungry, and I know how much you like lentil and goat-meat stew. I made it especially for you—I've actually been working on this meal for several hours."

"What's your point?" Esau growled.

"Well, isn't it true that I've often done this for you?"

"Yes," Esau replied grudgingly. "Spending all your time in the house with Mother, I suppose you have to do *something* to earn your keep," he finished with a sneer.

Jacob seemed not to hear Esau's belittling tone. He lowered his face to the bowl of stew in his hands, breathing deeply of the tantalizing aroma.

"Ahh, Esau, this has got to be the best batch yet."

"I'm sure it is. Now how long must I wait to taste it? Must I take it from you by force?" Esau took a menacing step toward Jacob. "I don't want to hurt you, Jacob!"

"No, no, of course not," Jacob replied, bowing his head. "But...I'd just like to ask a tiny favor of you."

"What?"

Jacob didn't answer right away. He looked away from Esau for a moment, his gaze roaming over the countryside. His eyes took on a dreamy look again as they settled on Esau.

"What! What is it you want me to do? You'd better tell me quick, before I swoon from hunger!"

Jacob took one pace backward and said, "Sell me your birthright, and you can have this bowl of stew—and the rest of it in the pot if you want."

The words thudded between them like a boulder from the sky. Jacob's steady gaze never wavered. He gently moved the bowl closer to Esau.

Esau looked from the face of his scheming brother to the bowl of stew and back again. He salivated, stomach rumbling.

My birthright? What good is my birthright if I die of starvation this day? And besides, no one need know about this. Jacob can have the family authority. And Father will still give me his blessing when it's time—the blessing of the older son. I'll have all the wealth.

61

He nodded and reached for the bowl.

"All right, brother. You can have my birthright. Here's my hand on it."

As they shook hands, the bowl of stew went to Esau and the birthright went to Jacob, forever changing the brothers' destinies.

In the twenty-first century, the birthright has gone the way of the dinosaur, replaced by wills and trusts. In ancient Israel, the birthright was both practical and spiritual. The eldest son became the head of the family upon the death of the patriarch, with all legal and spiritual control conferred upon him. Such a privilege was nothing to sneeze at nor take lightly.

Esau proved his disqualification to own the birthright and blessing when he disdained it for a bowl of soup. He reckoned, again, without Jacob's scheming nature when he convinced himself he'd still receive Isaac's blessing as the oldest son—Jacob later managed to trick him out of that also. Esau was left with the weakest of blessings imaginable in Jewish culture.

Esau's impulsive decision that day led to a lifetime of disobedience and rebellion and cemented future hostilities in the family. The world today still reels from his hasty decision, made as he squared off with his twin over the cook pot. He exchanged the eternal for the temporal, choosing immediate gratification over a lifetime of God's blessings.

For what bowl of soup would you trade your spiritual inheritance? You're probably not considering lentil and goat-meat stew, but what is tempting you this moment to take that first step away from the blessing of God's presence and work in your life?

- An opportunity to make more money in a career not of God's choosing?

- Marriage to a great guy or gal—but who does not profess Christ? Or perhaps he or she does profess Christ, but there's no visible fruit?

- Loving *yourself* so much that you permit yourself to hate another who has hurt or disappointed you, leading you to sever a relationship without God's blessing to do so?

- A harsh trial that you'd gladly escape at the first exit ramp, rejecting God, who shapes your character *through* the fires he allows?

I have stared at this same pottage, tempted just like you, and have traded God's presence for it, not considering the consequences. Those consequences now rear their ugly heads from time to time, bringing with them the excruciating pain of regret. *If only...*

But God is good. I look back and see how God protected me from other bowls of stew, blocked my reach, and reminded me to choose the eternal over the temporal. And sometimes I did.

Dear reader, do you smell that? It's the lovely fragrance of God's presence. Choose that, instead, over the next bowl of rotting pottage offered you—and I will, too.

For what have you traded the presence of God in your life? Financial success? Safety? Climbing the ladder of success? Peace and tranquility in your home?

Will you go back to where you were when God found you and start again, seeking only the pearl of great price—God's intimate and loving presence in your soul, allowing nothing to separate you?

Chapter 5
Eye Spy

*But Isaac said, "Your brother was here, and he tricked me.
He has taken away your blessing."*
~Genesis 27:35

Jacob squatted just outside the tent, listening. He'd honed the skill of eavesdropping to a fine art as a youngster. A young man now, it was still his primary method of finding and using the angle in any family situation to his best advantage.

His aged father, Isaac, called for the twin. Jacob quietly positioned himself so he could poke his head in and watch.

"Esau! My son, where's my son?" the blind man shouted, his hands curled like claws, groping the air.

Rebekah hurried to his side.

"My lord, what is it? Why do you shout? Are you ill?"

"Ah, my wife, my sweet Rebekah. You are ever watching for my needs. I'm no more ill than usual. I'm dying and would have my eldest son at my side."

Jacob stood then and moved closer to the tent folds, eyes peering through the opening.

Is he really dying? Why does he not call for me? I'm his son too.

"My lord, he's inspecting the new lambs not far away. I believe he took that young son of Amoz with him. I will bring him to you with all speed, husband." Rebekah rushed out of the tent. Jacob hastily backed away and around the corner.

He stood for a moment, watching his mother disappear over the first hill. He considered what he'd heard. He then turned his steps to the desert path leading away from the community. He wanted to think about his next move. His mother would be gone for a while, and then surely Esau would bathe before coming into their father's presence. He had time. He headed for the outer boundary of their settlement, to a favorite place he'd discovered where he would be quite alone.

Arriving, he paced, thinking deeply.

Hmm, this could be interesting. If he's truly dying, Esau may gain some advantage. I must be on my toes. I have his birthright, sold to me fair and square, though Esau hates me bitterly for it. He still won't admit it's his fault he lost it.

He had always judged Esau a dullard compared to himself. But it was never wise to discount his twin's fierce ambition, though it didn't match his own. Jacob always enjoyed the story of their birth—Esau was born first, his place as elder brother assured—but Jacob had made his presence felt from the first moment, grasping his brother's heel. And still, Jacob knew that Esau lived his life looking over his shoulder, always feeling the grip of Jacob's hand on his heel.

There was also the prophecy. *And your older son will serve your younger son.*

It had been a mantra with him since he was young and his mother had let it slip one evening as they'd sat around the campfire. At the time, he'd not understood it and had inquired privately of his mother the meaning. She had, perhaps unwisely, explained to him that someday he would ascend over Esau's place in the family—God had promised it.

He'd turned that over in his young mind, unable to grasp how that could possibly come about. But he'd repeated the prophecy in his mind each night as he was falling asleep. He'd tried, as a youngster, to keep his prospects to himself and not lord it over Esau, but there were a few incidents.

Of course, Esau also knew the prophecy, but he'd always disdained the possibility of Jacob ever usurping his place. Esau was much taller and stronger than Jacob, and he enjoyed his physical prowess. Through the years he'd shown Jacob how futile it was for him to expect the prophecy's fulfillment. Esau had bullied him unmercifully—catching him unaware, he would push his face into the sand or throw sheep manure at him—whenever he could do so without being caught. If their parents did happen to find out, the animosity between the brothers would be played out in the parents. Isaac would staunchly support Esau, and Rebekah would stand by her younger son. Jacob remembered how fiercely his parents argued.

One incident came to his mind now as Jacob paced. Esau had taunted Jacob in front of his friends, bringing Jacob to such a fury that he'd launched himself at his older brother, fists flailing. Somehow, Jacob had gotten the upper hand and knocked Esau to the ground. Jacob straddled him, Esau and his friends laughing uproariously. Jacob leaned close to Esau's face and shouted that one day Esau would be his slave, so he'd better watch out lest he find himself shoveling sheep dung for the rest of his miserable days.

The next moment, Jacob was on his back staring at Esau's massive knuckles—so close to his face the red hairs tickled his nose.

"You shut your mouth, little brother, or you'll be *eating* sheep dung from my shovel!" he'd shouted.

Esau had stood then and kicked sand in Jacob's face, joined by his friends. They'd laughed at him, calling him foul and humiliating names. After that, Jacob never again spoke the prophecy out loud.

His face burned now at the memory. Jacob decided then and there to employ his spying talents when Rebekah returned with Esau. As he walked back to camp, he schemed how he could somehow make God's prophecy come about—half of it was already his with the manipulated sale of Esau's birthright. Now he needed the elder brother's blessing before Isaac died.

How to do it, that is the question. Father may be blind, but he's not stupid. And he loves Esau with a passion equal to Mother's love for me. I must tread warily. I must listen closely and be quick to take every opportunity. If I make sure I'm in the right place at the right time, I will gain the advantage. After all, God promised.

As Jacob approached the tent, he saw Esau in the distance, running with his bow into the desert hills surrounding the camp. Rebekah beckoned from the tent door.

"Listen," she whispered, her mouth close to his ear. "I overheard your father say to Esau, 'Bring me some wild game and prepare me a delicious meal. Then I will bless you in the Lord's presence before I die.'"

The blessing! Just what I've been waiting for. This is my chance. How can I use this information to my advantage?

Jacob reckoned without his mother's lineage—her brother was Laban, who was well known for his duplicitous tactics. Rebekah already had a plan brewing for her beloved son's benefit.

Jacob listened as his mother unfolded her quickly hatched plan to steal the blessing of the elder son from Esau. She had it all worked out in her mind, and with but a few questions that Rebekah answered, Jacob agreed to it.

***

Late that morning, Esau had not yet returned. Jacob had done exactly what Rebekah had commanded and slaughtered two young goats. Rebekah quickly prepared them just the way his father liked, the way Esau would.

Jacob stepped inside, now wearing Esau's clothes. "Mother, is the food is ready for Father? I think we must hurry. Esau will surely be back soon."

"Yes, it's ready. Come here," she commanded.

Leaving Your Lover

She held up the skins she'd been working on, draping them over his arms and hands and across the back of his neck. Securing them in place, she stepped back to study her handiwork. The skins were rough on his neck, and Jacob put up a hand to scratch.

"No, my son," she said, staying his hand. "Don't touch it. It might slip and give us away. If your father finds out what we've done, it will be very bad for you—and for me, I'm afraid."

"Yes, Mother," he replied, "I'll remember. But I don't know if I can pretend to be Esau for very long. What if I can't convince him?"

"Don't worry. He's blind and practically deaf. And if I come in and casually call you Esau, he will be convinced. Now, are you ready? Remember what I told you."

Jacob nodded, still nervous, but by now he was desperate to get this over with and be assured of his success. This was the only way. Otherwise the prophecy would just be words in the elders' mouths.

He ladled some goat meat into a bowl and went into the inner chamber. His father immediately sat up.

"Esau, is that you? I can smell the meat. Come closer, my son."

Jacob placed the bowl next to his father. The steam rose from it, carrying with it the savory aroma his father loved. He knelt next to the cushions and waited.

"Why don't you speak, my son? *Are* you Esau?"

Jacob hesitated. Lying had never been a problem for him, but this was his father, and the lie now stuck in his throat.

What if—

Isaac drew back abruptly. "Speak, my son. I command you. I must know if you are Esau. The smell is that of my older son, but I must be sure. My time grows short, and I must give the blessing."

"Yes, Father," Jacob stammered, "it is I, Esau. I couldn't speak because it's so hard for me to think of you dying." There. It was done.

Isaac's face softened. "My son, you know to whom I go, and you will see me again. Give me your arm. I must feel your skin."

Jacob placed his hand in his father's. The old man's grip was still strong. Isaac ran his other hand up Jacob's arm, over the hairy skins his mother had made him wear. He then reached up to the back of Jacob's neck and pulled his head closer, sniffing. He let go and fell back on the cushion.

"Ahh—yes, it is you. I'd know that smell anywhere. You smell like the desert in bloom and feel like the animals you hunt so well. But how were you able to hunt and come back so swiftly?"

The next lie came out more easily than the first and with less guilt attached.

"Your God caused it to cross my path and made my aim sure."

Rebekah said from the doorway, "Ah, Esau, you have returned. And you have made your father his dinner. I'll leave you two alone."

"Yes, my love, he has returned. And none too soon! I'm ravenous."

She winked at Jacob and went out.

Jacob relaxed. It was going as Mother had planned.

"Father, would you like to eat now? I will help you."

"No, not yet. It will keep. I would tell you a story first. Then I must give you my blessing, now, while it's fresh in my mind. God has given me the words. Come closer." Isaac sat up a little straighter.

Jacob leaned in, Isaac's two hands gripping his own as his father lifted his weathered face upward.

"When I was but a sprout, my father, Abraham, took me to the hills. Do you remember this story, my son?"

"Yes, Father. You have told it many times." Jacob tried to keep the boredom out of his voice.

"God was testing your grandfather's faith in him. You will be tested, my son. Your mother and I have trusted Abraham's God all our lives. He has never let us down."

Isaac paused, taken by a coughing fit. Jacob waited anxiously, one ear cocked for sounds of Esau's return. He turned his head slightly and saw his mother listening in the shadows, just outside the fold of the tent. He turned his attention back to Isaac, lifting a cup of water to his lips. His father drank noisily, then cleared his throat and began again.

"Esau, my son, my time is short, and I cannot leave and go to God until I am assured that you understand your duty. You must make a decision whom you will serve—yourself and the pagan gods who surround us, or the God of your ancestors."

Oh, this is getting complicated! Jacob thought. *How am I to answer him?*

"Your mother and I sense that you waver. You must not waver."

Jacob was silent, wrestling with his conscience.

"Esau, you will have many opportunities as head of this family after I'm gone. But you must love God alone with all your heart. You must not marry outside his people—else you will be tempted to worship other gods. You must teach your family to worship God. And if you do all these things, when you come to your deathbed and *your* eldest son sits before you to receive your blessing, you will have no regrets. Do you understand, my son?"

"Yes, father," Jacob whispered.

"Good. When you leave my presence this day, you must leave with that conviction in your heart. But back to my story." Isaac lay back, a dreamy expression settling on his face.

"As we walked to the mountain so long ago, I asked your grandfather where the sacrifice was. He told me God would provide his own sacrifice. But when we arrived, we saw no sacrifice—only the dry hills surrounding us. My father and I looked into the brush and ravines but saw no ram or other animal, not even a dove in the sky. When we returned from our hunt, Father and I gathered wood for the fire.

"Still, we waited for the bleat of sheep or goat, but none came. Father—I can see it to this day—walked away from the camp and stood facing away from me, his shoulders and head bowed. I could hear him weeping, but I knew not why. As the sun sank behind the mountain, he came back to me and knelt before me. He hugged me and prayed, asking God to take care of me and lead me all of my life.

"He lifted me in his arms and placed me on the wood. He tied me down and raised his dagger over me. And suddenly I understood. He was going to sacrifice *me* for this God of his! That was why there was no ram. Esau, my son, can you put yourself in my place for a moment? I realized in that moment this one thing—that my father's God was so important to him that he would even slay his own son if he commanded it."

Jacob hunched over before his father, recalling the many times he'd told this story to his sons—but never with this passion. His own hypocrisy burned in his heart.

"I can still see father's face as he raised the knife. He wept. His arms and hands were shaking. At first, as I looked up at him, I didn't think he'd really do it. But now I believe he would have." Isaac's voice had dropped to a whisper. "He would have." Then, to himself, "Would I?" Isaac shook himself out of his reverie.

"Esau, your grandfather was right. God did provide his own sacrifice that day, and here I sit, an old man, as proof of it. My son, whom will you follow? Your mother and I must not leave this earth knowing our eldest son wavers between gods."

Jacob spoke through the rock in his heart and the lump in his throat. "I will follow your God, my father. I will now call him my God."

Jacob's heart raged as he saw the look of utter peace settle over Isaac's countenance. He pushed his guilt as far down as he could, down into the depths of his soul, where it would not bother him.

Leaving Your Lover

It must be this way. I must have his blessing, and he must go to his grave in peace, thinking Esau sits before him, promising to follow his God. It's the only way.

Isaac then straightened up and raised his hands to heaven. Jacob held his breath and waited.

This is it.

As Isaac spoke, Jacob heard a faint rustle behind him—his mother had moved away from the opening, clearly content that their mission was accomplished.

"From the dew of heaven and the richness of the earth, may God always give you abundant harvests of grain and bountiful new wine. May many nations become your servants, and may they bow down to you. May you be the master over your brothers, and may your mother's sons bow down to you. All who curse you will be cursed, and all who bless you will be blessed."

Isaac's head dropped back to the cushions, and he was almost instantly asleep, spent with the effort. Jacob rose and tiptoed out, raising a fist in the air. It was done. There was nothing Esau could do about it now.

As he closed the opening behind him, he heard Esau outside, arriving from the hunt and shouting to the servants to help him unload his kill and start a fire. Jacob turned and saw his mother sitting on her stool in the waning light, watching him expectantly.

"Yes, Mother, it is done."

Her eyes gleamed. She rose from her seat and stood in front of him.

"Mother, I…I…are you sure…" he whispered.

She put a finger to his lips to stay his words. "Yes, my son, I am sure. Now put it out of your mind."

They stood for a long moment, locked in a stare in the dim light, listening to Esau noisily preparing a meal for Isaac. Then Jacob turned abruptly and slipped out the back of the tent.

He walked the path again to his thinking place. He felt guilty, terribly guilty about deceiving his father and brother. As he gained the secluded place, he allowed himself to sink to his knees. Then he lay with his face in the dirt. He lay there until the sun had set and the cool breezes floated over his shoulders and he had assuaged his guilt by remembering he had only obeyed what his mother wanted. He lay there until he heard a great wail rise up in the desert—Esau crying over the stolen blessing.

And the rest, as they say, is history. Once again, Jacob the *leg puller* did an end run around God, and in his human finiteness made sure that infinite God kept his promise. Ably assisted by his mother, Jacob did by trickery and deception what God would have done anyway—in His holy, righteous, and uncomplicated way.

The result? Thousands of years of nation against nation, tribe against tribe, family against family, brother against brother—which continues today. We cannot know what would have happened if Jacob and Rebekah had let God be God and do it his way.

And of course, there's us. We think and think, we pace, scheme, plot, and manipulate our lives and the people in them to make sure we get what we want.

I have been that schemer, that leg puller, wanting so badly the things God wanted to give me anyway, *in his time*, that I did it my way, leaving the Lover of my soul on the outside of my heart looking in. And I've been grieving those sins ever since. I've learned the hard way that regret is food never eaten alone—it's always shared with the next generation, becoming more decayed and rotten with each passing decade.

While we busily remake life to suit ourselves, God is on his throne, waiting for us to kneel and ask for his blessing and plan.

He's there now, his gentle hand extended, longing to fill our lives with himself.

Will you join me there now and take what his gracious, merciful, and loving will has to give us? If we meet there and submit to his plan in his way, how sure our steps, and how peaceful and fruitful our earthly lives will be.

Perhaps you haven't yet acted on it, but what is enticing you now to take shortcuts to the destination you know God has for you?

Will you wait patiently for God to take you where he wants you to go?

Chapter 6
Samson and the Spy

But he didn't realize the Lord had left him.
~Judges 16:20

The knock was soft and insistent. She rose from her cushions, stepped swiftly to her door, and opened it a crack. She peered out at the group of seven armed men crowding her doorway.

"Yes? What is it you want?"

"You know what we want, woman. Let us in, and quickly, before we are noticed."

She giggled and held the door open for them, fingers sparkling with jewels.

"It wouldn't be the first time men were noticed congregating around my door. Please come in, and state your business plainly. My young servant told me you have a business proposition for me—and not the usual one, I gather."

They pushed their way in, making the small, luxurious room even smaller. She noticed two men on the fringe of the group ogling her. She ignored them. She knew why they were here, and it was not for that. She correctly identified the leader of this company and addressed her question to him, her silken outer wrap swishing about her bare feet.

"Well? Tell me about this 'arrangement' you wish to make with me. And it'd better be worth my while," she warned.

"Are you…alone?" he asked, scanning the room. He went to a curtained doorway, hand extended to pull aside the expensive hanging, but was stopped when Delilah pushed in front of him. She pushed his hand away.

"That room is my private sanctuary, and no one enters. No one," she insisted. "We are quite alone. I gave myself the night off in honor of your visit." She held the curtain aside so he could see the room was empty, then dropped it. He nodded and retreated to a position near his men.

She smiled craftily and seated herself on the nearest cushioned settee, gracefully spreading her colorful robes around her like peacock feathers. She leisurely picked a fruit from the basket at her elbow and held it out. The leader shook his head impatiently. She bit into it, allowing the juice to run down her chin. She dabbed it away with a delicate napkin and looked up at him.

"Please, you may sit," she said graciously, motioning to a nearby couch. "I'm sorry I don't have room for all of you to sit. I'm unused to having so many men in the room at the same time," she added impishly, eyes sparkling with mischief.

Laughter tittered among the men as they politely moved back and positioned themselves around the room, boots heavy on the floor, weapons clanking.

"You come with so many swords and knives, sir. Did you think I'd attack you? Actually, that might be fun," she murmured.

"You see before you, Madam Delilah, the rulers of your people. Some respect is in order," the spokesman said.

"I know very well who you are, some more than others," she said cryptically, gazing at two men in particular.

"Never mind that, woman," he said uncomfortably. "My name is Ekosh."

Delilah held out a limp hand for him to kiss. He leaned over and roughly touched her skin with his lips, then backed away and sat.

"And you are not 'my people,' sir. I have no people. I answer to no one."

"Only to the one who holds the most coin in his hand, I'll warrant," he said pointedly.

"And have you coin?" she asked coquettishly, lashes brushing her painted cheeks. "For me?"

"Yes, yes, we'll get to that." He leaned forward, his eyes never leaving hers.

He said the last thing she would have expected.

"I want to talk to you about the man Samson. We must capture him. And we need your help to do it."

Barely controlling her shock, she gazed at him under half-closed lids. *Samson? What do they want with him?*

"I'm unfamiliar with this name," she answered lazily, eyes carefully averted. She smoothed her robe with a trembling hand, then clutched it in her fist to hide her emotion.

"Come now—you know exactly who I'm talking about. My men here have observed him coming and going from this very room on many a night."

"You've been spying on me!" she accused. "How dare you! My business is no one else's. I've a mind to report you to your superior."

She tossed her long, elaborately dressed hair and stood abruptly. She walked slowly to the window and stood with her back to them. She knew her feminine curves were silhouetted against the window, and she could feel the soldiers' stares raking her back. She'd chosen this fitted dress carefully, as it showed her alluring body to its best advantage. It covered her completely over her bodice but plunged to the small of her naked back, draping in folds over her hips before falling to her sandaled feet. It had never failed to get the price she asked.

"Now don't pout, woman. We still haven't made our proposal to you—and it's quite a lucrative one."

Delilah, far from pouting, thought furiously. Her scheming mind had already settled on her course, but it wouldn't do to appear too eager. She must appear reluctant and make them beg, something at which she was skilled.

I must take the advantage. But Samson—no harm must come to that delicious man. I will find a way to take their money and keep him safe.

It was a titillating position in which she found herself. She waited a moment longer, then turned, one finger entwined in her hair.

"Hmm...Samson, you say? Yes, I do remember him. Samson, who a short time ago plucked the gates of Gaza out of the sand and carried them on his shoulders to Hebron? That Samson? The one who killed a thousand of your own soldiers with the jawbone of a donkey? Heavens, they named a hill after him! The Samson who ripped a lion apart with his bare hands? You want me to help you capture him? You might find the task of caging him just a bit beyond you and your soldiers." She snickered. "How much wine have you had this evening, sir?"

"None, madam. Now just listen. There's some secret to his strength—there must be—and if we can determine what it is, we'll have him. All you have to do is...well, what you usually do...and get him to tell you. What can be so hard about that? I'm sure you've weaseled such information out of men before, hmm?"

"What I usually do? What I usually do has nothing to do with beguiling secrets out of men. What I usually do is much simpler than that." She looked around the room at the company of leering men. "And what is to be my compensation? It'd better be no paltry sum."

"Each of us here in this room are prepared to give you eleven hundred pieces of silver."

Delilah's sculpted black eyebrows rose to her hairline in astonishment.

A measure of their desperation, methinks!

"There are seven of you! You will give me seventy-seven hundred pieces of silver?"

Leaving Your Lover

"Only if you drag his secret out of him and it works. Only if he becomes like a normal man. Not until," Ekosh answered.

The room was silent as a tomb as Delilah considered. All eyes were on her as she put her hand to her chin, index finger tapping her cheek.

This will never work. His strength cannot be taken away—how could it be? I will go along with them, take their money, and Samson will kill them. What could be easier?

Into the silence tiptoed her servant, a mere girl. She stopped abruptly in the doorway, eyes wide, taking in her mistress facing off with a roomful of men. The man nearest the door grabbed the girl by the nape of the neck. She squirmed, and he clutched her more tightly. His eyes roamed over her slight form.

"Well, well, who do have we here? Your apprentice, Mistress Delilah? Are you teaching her everything you know?"

Delilah stepped swiftly to the girl's side, jerking her out of the man's grasp and slapping him hard across the cheek. Her pointed fingernails raked his cheek, leaving trails of blood. He grabbed her by the arm and brought her close, pinning her arm behind her painfully.

"Sir," he said quietly, clearly enjoying her body struggling against him, "may we teach her some manners?"

The commander had a knife to his man's throat before he even knew it was coming.

"Leave off! This is not why we're here. Leave off, I say, or I'll slice your throat where you stand," he growled.

The man finally let go of her, and Delilah turned and pushed the young girl to the doorway.

"Leave us," Delilah said quietly.

The girl turned and fled, the slap of her bare feet echoing down the hallway.

Delilah closed the door quietly and turned, rubbing her arm. She stared the man down, and he finally moved back to his place.

"Well? Must we take our silver elsewhere?" Ekosh demanded.

"No, you may put it right here. I'll do as you say. But he," she said, pointing at the troublemaker, "he must have no part of this. If I see him near me or my servant, the deal's off. Do I make myself clear?"

"Yes, of course. I'll kill him myself if he gives any further trouble," he said with a pointed glare in the soldier's direction.

"Where is the money? You can leave it here when you go."

"I told you, when the job is done and we have him," Ekosh countered.

"Then let me at least see it. I will not be made sport of. I will see it—now—or you will leave without a deal." She was used to the ability to wind most men around her little finger, but the power she now felt over these men was intoxicating. She'd even enjoyed the sparring between the commander and his man.

Ekosh flicked a hand to the men behind him, and one came forward drawing a heavy leather bag from his cloak.

"Open it and show her," Ekosh commanded.

The man pulled the drawstring and stretched the mouth of the bag wide. Delilah peered inside. She looked up at Ekosh and smiled. She offered her hand to him, and he took it.

"Deal," she said softly. "How shall I notify you when I have weaseled, as you say, his secret out of him?"

Ekosh outlined the plan he had in his mind. Delilah considered his words carefully.

"Yes, it'll work. I'll send my servant to you when I have it. Then you and your men can hide nearby and capture him."

"Good. We will leave you now. See that the plan works, or you may lose more than the silver," he threatened. He turned and led his men out.

Delilah felt the first chill of fear. But she remembered the gleam of silver and tossed her curls nonchalantly. With her cunning and Samson's strength, this would be child's play.

***

Leaving Your Lover

"Why are you so angry, my love?" Samson asked sleepily, languishing upon her cushions. His large frame dwarfed the bed. His muscled arms flexed as he propped up the pillow behind his head. He raised up on one elbow and turned toward her.

She lay on her back, arms crossed over her bosom. His forefinger traced the curve of her cheek, straying down to throat and bosom. He leaned over and kissed her lips. She pushed him away, putting a cushion over her face.

"That you could ask that!" Her voice was muffled behind the cushion.

He fell to his back again, eyes closing.

Delilah dropped the cushion. She arose from his side and stomped—there was no other word for it—stiff-backed to the window.

Samson watched her under half-closed lids. Even in anger, turned away from him, she was the loveliest creature Samson had ever seen. She clenched and unclenched her fists, foot tapping, every muscle taught with tension. Her anger was just as seductive as her loving.

"Come, my love. Come back to me now and tell me why you are angry," he cajoled tenderly.

She turned to face him. The set of her mouth told him she was not buying his contrived innocence. He rose from the bed and came close, reaching large hands for her waist, but she moved just out of his grasp. *At any other time, this would be playing hard to get*, he mused. He dropped his hands.

"I was just playing, Delilah," he said, deciding to come clean. "You have to admit, it was great fun playing those Philistines for the fools they are."

"And me, you oaf! Have you forgotten that?" She turned away from him then and covered her face with her hands.

"Oh, Samson...how can you say you love me when you won't share your secrets with me? Isn't loving someone supposed to mean sharing—of secrets and dreams?" Her shoulders shook.

Samson was immediately contrite. "Delilah, look at me."

She didn't move. Samson grasped her shoulder, turning her to face him. He pried her hands away from her face, reddened with weeping.

"Delilah, Delilah, my love, don't cry. You've been after me for days and days. Don't you understand? I dare not reveal the secret. If I did and it fell into the hands of my enemies, now where would I be? As weak as any normal man."

"So you say! You think I'd tell? You don't trust me!"

"Don't play *me* for a fool! You've already repeated my lies three times. And three times they were lying in wait for me. Why should I believe you wouldn't reveal the truth if I told you? You're just like my wife, Timnah, pouting over a riddle. Now you, weeping and wailing, plaguing me to give up my secret."

"But, Samson, I knew you were teasing me all along, don't you get it? I was playing your game. And I care not that you mention her again to me. She's gone."

"But you just told me I'd played you for a fool along with the Philistines. Which is it, Delilah?" he asked sternly.

She smiled at him, the smile that always melted his resolve.

"I was just trying to make you feel guilty. I knew all along. Do you really think I'm that gullible?" She grasped his massive arms and shook him.

"I won't tell, Samson. I would never want these lovely arms to shrink and look like the sticks other men wear."

Samson searched her face and could see no deception—or chose to see none. But still he hesitated. He shook his head and turned to take his leave.

She ran ahead of him to the door and blocked it. He towered over her, looking down into her face, still wet with tears.

"Now what, Delilah?"

She buried her face in his chest, arms wrapped around him. He reached down and lifted her chin.

"Samson, don't you love me?" Her voice was as weak as a newborn lion cub. His heart dissolved. He leaned over and kissed her passionately.

"Of course I love you. But I must go now. I'll see you tomorrow, Delilah."

***

"Why do you spend so much time with that prostitute, sir? Do you intend to marry her?" Samson's chief servant inquired the next day. They sat together in Samson's private chamber, which he'd had built at the back of his father's home after his parents died. He'd designed it for his own comfort, two rooms large enough that he didn't feel cramped.

"I've tried marriage, my friend, and look where it got me. No, I don't intend to marry her—today." He grinned at Rafal. They'd been together for more than twenty years and could almost read each other's minds.

"Perhaps you should turn your attention and massive strength back to our Philistine masters instead of chasing after this woman. You know that when you are not with her, others are."

Samson narrowed his eyes and waved a hand in anger. Rafal clamped his lips together.

"And perhaps you should remember your place," Samson replied softly. "Or I'll turn my attention and massive strength upon you."

"I meant no disrespect, sir, but the rest of your household talks. And I've heard rumors in the market that some are disgruntled that you neglect counsel with the other leaders. They'd like to see you take the Philistine rabble to task like before. Samson, we've been under the boots of those dogs for forty years—we need you to rout them."

Rafal paused, then tried a different approach. "Remember when you burned their fields using three hundred foxes tied together by their tails?"

Samson smiled at the memory. "That was as much to punish my father for giving my wife away to my best man as to punish

Philistia, my friend," Samson said mildly. "Don't confuse the two."

"Again, a woman. They seem to complicate your life. Perhaps if you marry Delilah, she wouldn't hold so much sway over you."

Samson rose and went to the large window overlooking the town. He could see the valley of Sorek in the distance, where Delilah lived.

"No, my friend. It'd be more. And that's what I'm afraid of."

He strode to the door. Turning, he said, "I have some business I must attend to, Rafal—and yes, it's yonder, in the valley of Sorek. I'll see you tomorrow."

He went out. He knew he'd have to explain again to Rafal—tomorrow—why he went to her again. But his need of her trumped all else.

***

Delilah lay in the curve of his arm, triumphant eyes hidden under her veil. They'd played a game she'd devised. She'd received him dressed from head to toe in luxurious saffron robes with her head completely covered, pretending to be a stranger when he'd arrived. It added a spice to their lovemaking that Samson said he'd not experienced before.

She judged the time was right—he lay drowsily at her side, completely spent.

"Samson, my love," she said in a silky voice, "your strength is overpowering to me. I swoon when you take me in your arms. How come you to be so strong? Is it an elixir you take every day? Or is it by magic art? Tell me, please, my love. I want to know everything about you. No secrets between us, hmm?" She held her breath.

He turned toward her then, eyes still closed, and draped an arm over her waist.

"My hair has never been cut," he whispered into her ear. "I was dedicated to God as a Nazirite from birth. If my head were

shaved, my strength would leave me and I would become as weak as anyone else."

Delilah knew this was the truth, finally, and when he lay snoring, deeply asleep from the draught she'd given him, she sent her servant to Ekosh with a message.

Send the money. I have what you seek.

As soon as her servant returned with the money bags, she crept back to her bed with a manservant in tow, who carried a pair of large shears. He shaved off the seven locks of Samson's hair. Then the manservant beckoned to the doorway, where soldiers were waiting.

"Samson, wake up! The Philistines are here!"

***

Samson awoke from his deep sleep, jumping to his feet in a fighting stance. But something was tragically wrong, and Samson knew it immediately. He fell to his knees, weak and nauseated. Delilah backed away and ran out the door, spilling coin as she rushed from the house.

He reached up and touched his head, feeling nothing but rough stubble where his long braids had been. Then he knew.

The Lord has left me.

Rage overcame him, and he stood again and charged the soldiers as they surrounded him.

But they overpowered him easily. He looked around for Delilah, but she was gone. He was alone and helpless. He struggled against his captors, but they drove him to the floor and pinned him down, rough knees on shoulders and legs. A dagger suddenly gleamed in the dim light, poised above his face.

My God! I'm sorry! Please don't let this…

His plea ended in a strangled scream as the dagger plunged into his left eye. He fainted—and when he awoke, they had bound him with cords and chains of bronze, and carried him out, leaving his bloodied eyes behind on Delilah's floor.

***

"I'll see you tomorrow."

That tomorrow never came. Rafal learned the next day the fate of his friend, the great Samson. Now, months later, Rafal stood in the throng waiting for Philistine soldiers to parade Samson out. He craned his neck over the crowd, trying to get a glimpse. He'd heard rumors of what had happened—that the prostitute had betrayed Samson, that he'd been captured and forced to grind grain in the prison. That they'd blinded him.

The Philistines gathered today at their temple for a festival, a yearly celebration for their god, Dagon, which usually ended in drunken violence and debauchery, or so Rafal had heard. He'd never attended before, but today was different. A friend had told him yesterday that Samson would be on display today and that he'd be forced to perform for the crowd. Rafal waited in anguish, longing to see him, yet not wanting to.

Finally there was a great shout and Samson was led in, chained between four soldiers and walking next to a mere sprite of a servant who carried water in a jar. Rafal cringed when he saw the gaping black holes in his friend's face. His hair, now grown back, lay in filthy locks on the back of his neck. Samson looked hardly human, and Rafal lowered his head in a moment of grief.

They stopped for a moment, and the servant gave Samson a sip of water. Rafal saw Samson lean over and whisper something to the servant, who nodded and took Samson's hand, leading him to the large dais at the front of the temple courtyard.

Rafal judged there were more than three thousand in the crowd, many standing on the roof over the dais. The shouting intensified as Samson climbed the stairs.

"Dagon, Dagon, thank you for delivering our great enemy to us—he who slaughtered so many of us! He is now in our power, and weaker than the babe born yesterday!"

Leaving Your Lover

Rafal, finally sickened and unable to watch anymore, melted through the throng and, gaining the street, ran back to his home.

All is lost. We are to be enslaved by God's enemies forever because of our rebellion. And Samson, my friend...

***

Samson felt behind him and placed his hand on the pillar. The servant boy placed his other hand near the other pillar, then stepped back. Samson stood between the two pillars and drew himself up to his full height and raised both hands in the air.

The noisy crowd stilled, waiting breathlessly, watching the ripple of his muscles.

"Sovereign Lord, remember me just one more time. With one blow let me pay back the Philistines for the loss of my two eyes."

A titter of amusement traveled around the temple. Samson imagined some whispered behind their hands that the great Samson had become unhinged in the prison. Samson heard it, and a calm fell upon him. He stood quietly, waiting for the right time. Then the jeering and taunting began.

"Show us your strength, my lord Samson!"

"Can you see this, O great one?"

A melon hit Samson squarely in the face.

"Or this?"

A stone struck him on the knee.

Samson judged the time was right. The crowd was whipped into a drunken frenzy as they yelled and mimicked him. All that was left for him to do was the plan that had come to him in the night as he'd prayed to the God of heaven on his knees and repented of his past sins and passions.

"Let me die with the Philistines," he murmured.

Then he placed his hands on the two pillars on either side of him and pushed. The shouting died down as they watched him strain against the pillars. The masses on the roof looked down on his head, swilling their drinks and clapping each other on the shoulders.

Seconds later they heard the first mighty crack—and in the next moment the entire structure came down on their heads, bringing with it the hundreds on the roof. The temple of Dagon lay in ruins, Samson himself buried with thousands of God's enemies.

Samson leaps onto the stage of Israelite history, reminding us of a swashbuckling hero as he tears apart a lion's jaw with his bare hands. But as with all swashbuckling heroes, Samson has serious weaknesses. Despite his God-given position as one of the judges of Israel and the opportunity to deliver Israel from the Philistines, Samson instead is governed by his appetites. He loves God and wants to serve him, but he can't quite overcome his passions.

Samson's life is a life lesson to us. His massive physical strength was no match for temptation. It's not physical strength that will take us successfully through this dim life and into the blazing brilliance of God's home. It's faith in the awesome power of God—the same power that raised the Lord Jesus Christ from the dead.

Samson had counted on Samson his whole life. But at the end of it, when the chips were down, when all bets had been placed, when no more choices could be made, he realized that in spite of the size of his muscles, he couldn't wrestle and subdue his cravings. But God could. Those character weaknesses were no match for the power of God. Samson made his choice to follow God and rolled the dice. Better late than never. The Scriptures say he killed more on that one day than he had during his entire life.

The question we must answer is, who do we count on in this very moment? Will *we* live this life the way we choose, reserving

total dependence on God to our last moment clothed in flesh and blood?

What a wasted life that would be! Samson shouts to us from the above the clouds—*Follow God now!*

What weakness plagues you over and over, causing you to see yourself as a loser in the battle instead of a victorious warrior? How are you counting on yourself instead of God?

What must you do to turn that weakness into the power of God in your life?

Chapter 7
Bleat

Then what is all the bleating of sheep and goats and the lowing of cattle I hear?
~1 Samuel 15:14

"What are you doing, my king? Why do you burn the incense? Were you not to wait for the man of God to arrive?"

Saul raked his servant with a glare. The man stumbled backward, almost tripping over a rock.

"I am king over God's people. Samuel is just his servant. What is a prophet, a priest, or a judge compared to a king?"

"But...but..." his servant stuttered in confusion, staring at the golden bowl in his king's hand.

"Seven days have passed, and he is not here. Do you not see the fear in the eyes of my warriors? The Philistine barbarians are in Micmash—a quarter of a day's march away—and they will overwhelm us with their numbers."

"Yes, Lord, but you do wrong to burn the incense. It is the duty of the priest," his servant bravely admonished.

"My men slip away in the night, fool!" Saul bellowed. "Has that escaped your notice? If Samuel chooses to ignore his promise, I must, as king over Israel, step in. Our survival as a nation is at stake. Now get out of my way."

Shaking his head, the servant backed away from Saul, then turned and ran. Saul watched the retreating figure for a moment, then resumed his preparations. Soon the fragrance of the burning oil permeated the camp. Saul saw some of his men gazing curiously.

Let them stare. We must have God's blessing. And if Samuel neglects his duty, I, the king, surely will not!

Just as the smoke cleared from the burnt offering, Saul heard a step behind him.

"What is this you have done?"

"Samuel, my friend! At last you are here. I had given up hope that you would come in time." Saul hurried forward and bowed low before the priest.

Samuel did not answer the king. Lips tightening in a thin line across his face, he lifted his sad eyes to meet Saul's. Then Samuel's gaze lowered to take in Saul's robes covered by the priest's tunic he'd donned.

Panic crowded Saul's throat as his mind scrabbled for an excuse Samuel would accept.

"I...I...saw my men scattering from me, and you didn't arrive when you said you would. I have reports that the enemy is at Micmash ready for battle. What was I to do?"

Saul looked away, fidgeting nervously with the fringe of the ceremonial robe. Unaccustomed shame washed over him, and he hastily removed the robe, holding it out to Samuel. Samuel did not take it, putting his hands behind his back. Still, he said nothing.

"Samuel! You must understand—God's people are in mortal danger from the Philistine army. I realized the battle was upon us and I hadn't asked for God's help. So I felt compelled to offer the burnt offering myself before you came."

"You err, my son," Samuel replied quietly, sadness in his eyes. "God's people are *not* in mortal danger from the Philistines, because God is already here."

"But..." Saul began.

Seeing the hardness of Samuel's face, he lost his temper. "Samuel, *I* am charged with the safety of this people. That is my sacred duty, given to me when you—yes, you—anointed me king. You weren't here. I was. The nation's very existence was threatened. I had to burn the offering or risk annihilation by God's enemies. So don't stand there and shame me before my men!"

Saul was unprepared for the priest's answer.

Samuel gave a great sigh and looked heavenward, tears forming beneath his eyelids and slipping down his weathered cheeks.

"Saul, I passed by Carmel on my way here. Do you know what I saw?"

Saul was silent, suddenly wishing himself anywhere but here.

"I saw a monument to a foolish king. Who built it, Saul?"

Saul spread his hands wide and locked eyes with Samuel. "I did. I'm the king. I have a right to build monuments—even to myself if I so choose."

Samuel bowed his head, hands folded in front of him. "I knelt before that monument and begged God to be merciful to the king. I heard no answer from God."

"But, Samuel, my father—"

"How unwise you are, my son," Samuel whispered. "You are charged with obedience to God, and you have failed. *He* is responsible for the safety and prosperity of his people. You have completely misunderstood your duty—taught to you *by me* when I anointed you. You have not kept the command the Lord your God gave you. Had you kept it, the Lord would have firmly established your kingdom over Israel forever."

Saul blanched, unable to stop the trembling of his hands. *What is he saying?*

"But now your kingdom must end, for the Lord has sought out a man after his own heart. The Lord has already appointed *him* to be the leader of his people, because you have not kept the Lord's command."

"What are you talking about, Priest? *I* am king over Israel! By your own hand, I am king."

"No, my son, not by *my* hand—but by the Lord Almighty's hand. And now he has removed it."

Samuel turned and shuffled away, shoulders drooping. He left Saul enveloped in the lingering wisps of smoke from the burnt offering, clutching the priest's robe,

That evening Saul walked the starry hills outside the camp at Gilgal. He wondered if God had truly rejected him. He still remembered the joyous day when Samuel anointed him and how the people had cheered. Heat washed over him as he recalled how embarrassed he had felt at the attention. But he'd grown used to the people's adulation. They'd asked for a king, and God had given them one—himself. Why would God establish him as king and then take it away from him? It didn't make sense.

Samuel's getting old—he probably got it wrong. God just wanted him to remind me of my duty. And I am sorry about it. I should have waited for Samuel. I won't make that mistake again.

With those comforting thoughts settled in his mind, Saul squared his shoulders and returned to camp in a much better frame of mind, ready to plan his next campaign.

***

One day, Samuel came to Saul with a message from the Lord. Their relationship had never recovered the old affection, but Samuel was still Israel's priest and Saul was still Israel's king, and they must make the best of it.

"It was the Lord who told me to anoint you as king of his people, Israel. Now listen to this message from the Lord! This is what the Lord of Heaven's Armies has declared: 'I have decided to settle accounts with the nation of Amalek for opposing Israel when they came from Egypt. Now go and completely destroy the entire Amalekite nation—men, women, children, babies, cattle, sheep, goats, camels, and donkeys.'"

Leaving Your Lover

Saul, eager to please Samuel, immediately began preparations for the assault. He gathered his generals around him, and soon they were deep into planning war on the enemies of Almighty God.

Many days later, after the campaign against Amalek was completed, Saul was back at Gilgal, sitting with his generals and toasting their success. Agag, the Amalekite king, was tied up nearby, stripped of all but the barest of garments, bloodied and enduring taunts by the youngest soldiers in the camp. A singer retold the story of their victory, the ending stanza a beautiful description of the monument Saul had made for himself in Carmel. His soldiers regaled each other with battle stories, each one trying to outdo the others with tales of their courageous exploits. Saul leaned back against his chair positioned outside his tent, enjoying the scene before him. This is what he lived for, for his name figured prominently in the stories. His men knew well their king's appetite for praise and glory, so they bragged about him as much as they bragged about themselves.

A messenger, out of breath, suddenly made his way through the throng of drunken soldiers until he stood before Saul.

"Well, what news?" Saul demanded.

"My king, Samuel approaches. He says he will have speech with you."

"Samuel? Here?" Saul whispered nervously. He leaped to his feet and gave brisk orders to his servants. Then he prepared himself to greet Samuel. He sent his men and most of his generals away and changed his tunic, smoothing his hair and beard with shaky hands.

Why is he here? Why does he come now? Perhaps he has heard of our victory and comes to toast it with us.

He stepped outside his tent and made his way down the path to meet Samuel, trying to convince himself that the priest was here with accolades. He stopped, seeing Samuel approaching. He tried in vain to still his trembling hands, finally putting them behind his back.

When Samuel drew near, Saul greeted him with bluster and cheer.

"May the Lord bless you, Samuel. I have carried out the Lord's command!"

Samuel shuffled slowly until he stood right in front of the king, his cold eyes raking Saul up and down.

"Samuel, are you ailing? You look…haggard. And in the face of my victory. Come. Change those filthy clothes and have some wine, some food. Celebrate with us, my friend!"

"You have carried out the Lord's command? You have completely destroyed the enemy down to the last man, oxen, sheep, and dog? That is what you say to me and to God?"

"Y-yes," Saul stammered. Then stronger. "Yes, I did. The Amalekites are completely defeated. They will no longer trouble the Lord's people, Israel."

"Hmm…you use the word *defeated*, not *destroyed*. God's command to you was complete annihilation of the Amalekites."

"Words, just words, priest! The Amalekites are gone."

Samuel cocked an ear first in one direction, then another.

"Then tell me, Saul. What is all this bleating of sheep and goats and the lowing of cattle I hear?" Samuel thundered.

"Oh…ah…well, it's true the army spared the best of the sheep, goats, and cattle. But they are going to sacrifice them to the Lord your God. We have destroyed everything else."

Samuel's gaze drifted to Agag, tied to a thorn bush, and back to Saul.

"Is that so? You say 'The Lord *your* God' as if he is mine and not yours. I care not for those words, my son."

"Well…I…I…" Saul sputtered.

"Stop! No more of your foolish excuses. I'm sick to death of them."

Saul took a step backward, hand drifting to the sword hilt at his waist.

"Stay, Saul. Listen to what the Lord told me last night!"

Saul dropped his hand, perspiration dripping into his eyes.

And Samuel told King Saul the dreaded news. Saul tried to weasel out of Samuel's condemning accusation, but for the first time in his life his stature and handsome appearance counted for nothing.

"What is more pleasing to the Lord?" Samuel pressed. "Your burnt offerings and sacrifices or your obedience to his commands?"

Saul had no answer for that. He stood in the filthy rags of his victory, soul bared before Samuel and unable to explain himself.

"Listen!" Samuel continued. "Obedience is better than sacrifice, and submission is better than offering the fat of rams. Rebellion is as sinful as witchcraft, and stubbornness as bad as worshiping idols."

Samuel stepped back from Saul. Face working, clearly trying to control his grief, he ignored Saul's outstretched arm.

Samuel then turned his back on Saul and raised his face to the sky. Saul could just hear the priest's voice whispering words not meant for him—but to someone else.

"Why, my Lord? Must I say *that* to him? Must I? He has been like a son to me!" Slowly he turned and faced Saul again, arms trembling at his sides.

Saul tried again to make Samuel understand. He barely noticed the steely glint in Samuel's eyes.

"I'm sorry. I was only doing what the people demanded. Please forgive me and come back with me so that I may worship the Lord."

Samuel gathered his robes about him and drew himself up to his full height. The anointed king of Israel shrank before him.

"And now the shepherd blames the sheep for his own folly? No, this disaster is on you, Saul, not on your people. I will not go back with you. Since you have rejected the Lord's command, he has rejected you as king over Israel." Samuel turned to leave.

Frantic, Saul reached out and grasped Samuel's robe, tearing off a piece.

The two men stared at the piece of cloth as the night breezes swirled between them. Silence stretched as the cloth fluttered to the ground, landing between them on the cooling desert sand. Saul lifted his eyes to Samuel in mute appeal.

Samuel shook his head, then grasped his robes and shook them out as if trying to rid himself of some stain.

"The Lord has torn the kingdom of Israel from you today and has given it to someone else—one who is better than you. And he who is the Glory of Israel will not lie, nor will he change his mind, for he is not human that he should change his mind!"

It wasn't long before Samuel traveled back to his home in Ramah, but not before obeying God's command—the command Saul chose to disobey—to execute Agag. The Amalekite king was hacked to pieces by Samuel's own sword.

Saul returned to his home in Gibeah a victorious king but a defeated follower of God. Samuel and Saul were never to meet again, and Samuel mourned constantly for him until his death. Saul's life was filled thereafter with rebellion after rebellion, even consulting mediums—something expressly forbidden by God—his mind finally spiraling into madness.

Many years later, Saul was killed in battle on Mount Gilboa, along with three of his sons. The king of Israel ended his earthly life fastened to a Philistine wall, his dead body on gruesome display for all the world to see.

Saul would never know the future ramifications of his disobedience. Because he did not totally annihilate Agag's family, his descendants troubled Israel centuries later. Queen Esther came head to head with one—Haman the Agagite, who devised a plan to pay the Persian King Xerxes to murder every Jew in his kingdom. Thankfully, Esther counted obedience to

God more important than her own life, and she thwarted Haman's evil plot.

And God? The Scriptures say he was "sorry he'd ever made Saul king of Israel." What a sad commentary on a life!

Does God hear the bleat of your disobedience? Have you asked yourself if God has ever been sorry he made you? Put you where you are today?

I, for one, do not ever want to hear that from the Lover of my soul. I want to hear, "Well done, Deb! Come in and enjoy me forever." How about you?

What has God torn from your life because you refused to obey?

Will you kneel bravely now and ask God what he would have you do about that? Or will you continue on that same path that leads to utter defeat and soul emptiness?

Chapter 8
Fallen

*In the spring of the year, when kings normally go out to war,
David sent Joab and the Israelite army to fight…However,
David stayed behind in Jerusalem.*
~2 Samuel 11:1

"What? You're not going with us, my king?" Joab asked in surprise, his armor clanking noisily.

David looked up from the scroll he was studying and surveyed his nephew in the early morning light filtering through the windows.

"Why do you question me?" he asked, absently fingering the scroll. "You and your men can easily handle the end of this war with the Ammonites. And we've soundly trounced those Arameans, so that threat is eliminated."

"Yes, *we* have. That is my point. As always, you were with us at the head of your army. Your presence gives us strength. It surprises me that you would stay in Jerusalem when it's time to finish this," Joab replied, then hesitated. "And I don't know how the men will react, Sovereign," he added carelessly.

David drew himself up and thundered, "Do you think I should care how the men react to my command? I only care that I'm obeyed!"

Joab took a step back. "My king!" he said evenly, lowering his head and turning to go. The general made it to the door of David's inner chamber before he was halted.

"Wait, nephew. Come back."

Joab obeyed immediately, dropping to one knee in front of David. David laid a hand on Joab's head, bidding him rise.

"Look. I'm sorry I snapped at you. And I do care about my men—you know that," David said. "I just don't care to have my orders questioned, nor my men moping about because I choose to stay behind—*once*. There are things that need the king's attention right here in the city. And I need a rest, Joab. As I said, you and the men can handle it. Without the Arameans, Ammon is a ripe plum to be picked by Israel. God has told us—and *he* goes with you. You don't need me for this campaign."

David didn't care for the measured look in Joab's eyes. He laid a heavy hand on his general's shoulder and gave it a small shake.

"Now go, General, and the Lord of Hosts be with you."

David turned his back on Joab and stepped to the window.

"And send word to me of the battle. If I'm needed, I'll come."

"Yes, my king." Joab marched out.

David moved outside to the balcony, which overlooked the city. The sun peeped over the eastern desert horizon, casting its light over Jerusalem. He loved this time of day. His city was bathed in a golden glow, the surrounding sand glittering as with a million diamonds. The call of an eagle circling high above, the bleat of goats and sheep, and the early morning sounds of the city stirring never failed to flood his soul with gratitude at the mercies of God, who brought him to this place. But this day, that feeling of gratitude was marred. David felt unsettled in some way, and he couldn't put his finger on it—a faint feeling of self-doubt—as if he'd forgotten to do something important. He breathed deeply and stretched. His mind traveled back in time, to the beginning.

It seemed like yesterday he stood in shock and humility before Samuel, his lute clattering to the floor at his feet. He, David, the youngest and weakest of his father's sons, a filthy shepherd boy still smelling of sheep urine, was brought out of the fields and anointed the next king of Israel. His brothers

glared. His father all but sneered as his older, stronger sons were passed over. He remembered the next few days and weeks as his brothers took every opportunity to secretly tease and bully him—he'd tried to just stay out of their way.

He recalled the years of serving under Saul, playing the lute and singing songs of praise to God to soothe the madness that gradually overtook the king. Then came the years of hiding in caves and in the camps of Israel's enemies as Saul, rejected and replaced, sought to rid the earth of God's anointed king.

David allowed a tiny feeling of pride to crawl into his heart as he thought over the hardness of his life and how he'd overcome all of it to be standing here in his palace. His practiced self-discipline slipped for a moment, and he knew it immediately.

No, it wasn't me. It was the Lord who brought me here. At that thought, his pride slithered away.

He stretched slowly again, thinking of the days ahead—of quiet study and prayer, of visiting his wives, of music and poetry, of strolling through his city—the noise and dust of battle far away. He told himself he was glad of his decision, that he was in the right, and that battles could be won by good armies without the king in attendance.

David strode away from the balcony and headed for the palace gate, planning his day—but still the niggling worm of doubt burrowed in his mind and cocooned itself there.

Much later that day, in the waning light, David again watched from his balcony. He'd been to the barracks earlier and given last instructions to his generals and commanders. He'd proclaimed his confidence and encouragement to his men, reminding them that the Lord of Hosts rode at their head and would give them victory over the Ammonites at Rabbah. He promised to pray daily for their success. And then his mighty men, one by one, proclaimed their allegiance to the House of David, among them the Hittite. It had been a good day, and a long one.

Now as he watched from his balcony, his army marched out to the cheering of the crowds. The king noted many eyes turned his way, so he waved and pumped his fist at them. That gave impetus to their cheers—the deafening sound reverberated off the stone walls and echoed in the streets.

The Ammonites must surely hear, David thought. *Methinks they're shaking in their sandals even now, and when my army arrives at their gate, Israel will find the Ammonite nation fled.*

As the dust of marching feet settled and the last of his army disappeared into the valley, David stepped back into his sanctuary. He let out a long breath, allowing the peace and quiet to soak into his soul. Picking up a scroll, he settled at his desk to pen another stanza to the song he'd been writing.

> Why are the nations so angry? Why do they waste their time with futile plans? The kings of the earth prepare for battle; the rulers plot together against the Lord and against his anointed one. "Let us break their chains," they cry, "and free ourselves from slavery to God."

David thought deeply of this opening to his song. *How futile to oppose God and his plan. I must teach my people that to follow God is the best and simplest way to live.*

The scratching of David's pen continued into the night as he prayed for the words that would instruct his people to obey the Lord God and no other.

***

David spent the next morning with his ministers and advisers. They planned the next military campaign and discussed, rather heatedly, rumblings of discontent among his sons. It was a tiring morning, and the king determined he would take the afternoon hours off to play his lute and rest.

Leaving Your Lover

Late in the afternoon after an energizing nap, David ordered a meal brought to him. Good wine, lamb stew, and a sweet concoction of dates and nuts refreshed him. He sat back in his chair, wiping his lips with a napkin. Sipping the wine, he glanced at the two servants waiting nearby.

"My good men, you may clear the table. I won't require anything more tonight."

His servants leaped to obey, piling the dishes and leftover food high, and carried their armloads noisily out the door.

The light waned as David went out to his balcony and climbed the stairs to the roof, where he liked to think and pray. He paced, wondering how the battle went.

Adonai, go before them. Let not our enemy gain a foothold. Give wisdom to my nephew Joab as he directs the troops, and may we lose none. You have given them courage—increase it now so that the fame of your name, Lord God, would increase and your enemies would be brought low.

David stopped his prayer abruptly. The worm in his conscience burst from its cocoon and harried him. His muscles tightened and his head throbbed as he recalled Joab's surprise when told the king would remain behind. He rubbed a shaky hand over his forehead.

Why did you not go with your men to battle? You should be there. What if it goes badly?

David answered the worm. *No, I need rest in order to be at my best for the next campaign and to deal with my rebellious sons. Surely I'm entitled. I'm the king. I decide when and if. I decide who goes and who stays.*

And with David's silent argument, the worm crawled back into its nest and quieted.

David's muscles relaxed as he stepped to the parapet, one foot on the stone step as he leaned forward and stared over the rooftops. The light from the moon suffused the rooftops in a soft glow.

The moon rises early this night.

Looking down, the king's gaze was arrested by movement in his peripheral vision. Stepping to the right, he focused his stare on one particular rooftop close by. Eyes wide, David's jaw slackened at the sight that met his eyes.

She had her back to him in the bright moonlight, her naked skin beaded with water. Her dark hair swung loose and hung below her waist. A nearby servant held her robes.

David watched with burning fascination, palms slick.

Who is she?

The longer he watched, the more he needed to know. Burning fascination became burning desire. The king stood stone-like, trying to still his riotous thoughts. Strategies to take her chased themselves around in his mind, where a moment ago petitions to God for the protection of his army had lodged.

I could accidentally meet her in the marketplace. I could have her brought to me. I could innocently stroll past her dwelling—maybe she would make the first move once she saw me. I must find out who she is.

The worm answered his riotous thoughts.

This is wrong. You shouldn't be here. You should be with your army. You shouldn't be watching this woman. You have enough women. You are married. You are the king, blessed by the Lord God beyond measure. Your people watch you, listen to you, love you.

David brushed a hand over his eyes, shook his head, and tried desperately to silence the worm.

Do not take what is not given by him.

As the worm's voice rose insistently, it threatened to drown out David's stratagems. He frantically tried to escape the worm's voice, twisting and turning in his mind—but the view from every angle was the accusing worm.

The woman's servant stepped to her side and enfolded her in her robes. Her body was now hidden from David's sight. He gripped the stone parapet, muscles bulging with tension.

I must have her.

The worm started to answer him, but with a sudden movement, the king lifted his heavy boot-clad foot and crushed it, silencing it forever.

***

"You're what?" David's mind reeled. He'd received the message from her, and now she knelt before him, sobbing.

"What will we do?" she asked frantically, hands on her belly. "Uriah has not been near me in months, since you keep him on the battlefield."

He leaned over and patted the top of her head, then brought her to her feet. She kept her eyes downcast.

"Leave it to me. I'll figure something out," he whispered, not believing his own words. He motioned to his servant standing just out of earshot.

"See that she gets home," he commanded. Then, to her, "You can rest assured I, the king, will settle this issue for you. Thank you for bringing it to my attention."

As they disappeared around the corner, David heard an unwanted voice in his head. The worm he thought he'd crushed weeks ago now crawled out of the recesses of his mind, larger than ever. It rose up and swayed back and forth, its accusing eyes round and piercing his own.

Remember? I told you not to take what God has not given. Now you have a real problem—one you can't possibly hide from. It's not like you can...

Oh, shut up, you infernal creature! I have to think!

The worm fell silent. David strode to the door of his chamber, shouting for one of his secretaries to come to him.

The secretary approached and fell to one knee. "Yes, my lord, what can I do for you?"

"Send a message to Joab. Tell him to send Uriah to me—without delay."

The servant scurried out, and David sat down heavily on his chair, leaning over with his head in his hands.

What have I done?

***

Days later, David knew his plan had not worked. Uriah was an honorable man and could not be persuaded to sleep with Bathsheba before returning to the battlefield. Bathsheba had sent messages to the king, frantically asking when her husband would come to her. Her letters accused him, the king, of putting her in this compromising position. He knew well the punishment that might be in store for her, and he cringed at the thought. He read her last missive over again now.

"My lord, you have used your position to compromise me. I care not if you, in your kingly rage, have me killed for my words—but I beseech you, think of your child! He is innocent in this. You must send Uriah to me without delay that my child can be brought up in peace and safety."

David shook his head. He must tell her that Uriah was already preparing to go back to his men—that he refused to come to her, preferring not to enjoy the company of his wife when his men were deprived. He sat down and penned the message and gave it to the runner waiting just outside.

David sat with his head in his hands, discarding plan after plan until he was left with only one. He sat up, wiped his brow, and prepared another message. *Joab: Station Uriah on the front lines where the battle is fiercest. Then pull back so that he will be killed.*

David gave that message to another servant and told him to give it to Uriah to carry to Joab. Such was Uriah's honor that the king knew he would not open it.

Mind and heart churning with guilt, he wandered out to his balcony and gazed in sadness at the rooftop below where it had all begun. How had it come to this?

You know, said the worm.

Several days later a messenger arrived at the palace with a report from Joab. David grabbed it and dismissed the messenger. Opening it with shaky hands, he quickly read through it. His

scheme had worked. Uriah lay dead on the battlefield, and Bathsheba could now be brought to him after her period of mourning was over. David thought he'd feel relieved, calm.

He felt nothing.

***

"There were two men in a certain town," Nathan the prophet said to the king many months later. "One was rich and one was poor. The rich man owned a great many sheep and cattle."

"Nathan, what is this about? Another of your stories?" David asked, hands trembling in his lap.

"Let me finish, Sovereign. The poor man owned nothing but one tiny lamb. He raised that little lamb alongside his own children. It ate from the man's own plate and drank from his cup. He cuddled it in his arms like a baby daughter." Nathan paused.

David looked up. "Well, go on—you have my full attention."

"One day," Nathan continued, "a guest arrived at the home of the rich man. Instead of taking from his own herd to make a meal, he took the poor man's lamb and killed it." Nathan stopped, eyes locked on his king's.

David stood suddenly, throwing his chair backward with a mighty crash. He came swiftly around his desk to stand before Nathan.

"As surely as the Lord lives," he vowed, "any man who would do such a thing deserves to die! He must repay the poor man fourfold for what he stole and slaughtered with no pity."

Nathan crumpled before the king, falling to his knees, hands outstretched. David was astonished.

"Here, here, Nathan—it's only right this should happen. No one should be above the law."

Nathan rose shakily to his feet. He bowed his head and settled himself. Then, turning accusing eyes on his king, he threw out an arm at David.

"You are that man!"

David turned white, trembling from head to foot. Nathan wasn't finished.

"God has given you everything. He has withheld nothing from you. He says he would have given you much, much more. But now, why have you despised the word of the Lord and done this horrible deed? For you have murdered Uriah the Hittite with the sword of God's enemy, the Ammonites, and you have stolen his wife, his little lamb. You are judged by God, my king!"

David stumbled backward and caught himself by grabbing the edge of his desk. Bile rose to his throat, causing him to cover his mouth to keep from vomiting.

How does the prophet know?

Foolish question, answered the worm. *God knows your heart and informs his faithful prophet.*

"From this time on, your family will live by the sword because you have despised God by taking Uriah's wife to be your own. Because you killed Uriah with the sword of the Ammonite as surely as if you'd wielded it yourself, the sword will never leave your household. He will cause your own family to rebel against you. God will give your wives to another man before your very eyes, and that man will bed them publicly. You sinned secretly, but God will make this happen to you openly in the sight of all Israel."

The king of Israel fell prostrate before God's prophet and cried loudly, his fists pounding the floor.

"I have sinned against the Lord!" David's heart burst within his chest at the words. He sobbed at Nathan's feet, pouring out his repentance.

Nathan waited quietly until the king sat up. When David finally stood before Nathan again, his sight had shifted…a cloud lifted…his vision cleared. He took Nathan's hands in his own and knelt again and kissed them.

"Nathan, my friend, thank you for not withholding from me God's message, as hard as it was to hear it. It's surely true that God knows our hearts, and he has been waiting for this stubborn one of mine to soften. But since I was unyielding, he had to use his loyal servant, you, my friend."

Nathan bowed his head, touching the top of David's head. "God has forgiven you, my king. *You* won't die for this sin." He paused.

"I won't?" David asked, hope in his voice.

"No—your child will die. Because you showed utter contempt for the word of the Lord, his innocent life is forfeit."

David bowed his head and wailed his grief at the floor. Nathan turned quietly and left. David remained there for the remainder of the day and night, unable to rise. His men stood guard outside, allowing no one to disturb him.

David and Bathsheba's child fell ill with a deadly disease and died. They mourned him the rest of their lives. But that's not where it ended. Such sin visits itself on the next generation, and if allowed to flourish, always grows in scope and vulgarity.

His wise and beloved son Solomon fell prey to the enticements of pagan women, diluting the worship of God to a lukewarm mix of religions. Instead of the pure, passionate, fiery love for the Almighty and obedience to Him alone, Israel devolved into a divided nation whose identity as God's people was lost for centuries.

God graciously spared David from seeing this, but after the king died, it was a free-for-all between his sons. David's sin marked his family line for generations to come.

The next time we're tempted to think we sin in a vacuum, let's remember King David. His sin began with the choice to be where he shouldn't and ended with the deaths of two innocents and the fall of a nation. Though he repented and was mercifully forgiven, those consequences remain today.

One moment in time—on a balcony in Jerusalem—ended in adultery, murder, the death of an innocent child, and the spiritual decline of God's people.

Look ahead. Where will your *one moment in time* lead? Where will mine?

Think About It...

Are you poised to make a selfish decision that will affect your family for generations to come?

Will you pause long enough to picture what your children, grandchildren, and future generations will look like if you go ahead and gratify your self-seeking and self-promoting desires?

Chapter 9
As the Heart Turns

*Now King Solomon loved many foreign women...in
Solomon's old age, they turned his heart to worship other
gods instead of being completely faithful to the Lord his God,
as his father, David, had been.*
~1 Kings 11:1, 4

"Jedidiah, my son, come closer. I would have you with me at the end."

David's son immediately arose from his couch and approached the king. He loved it when his father called him by his God-given name—Jedidiah—"loved by the Lord." Most addressed him as Solomon, but David often used the other. It was an intimate endearment on his father's lips.

Solomon went to his knees before his father's bed, bowing his head almost to the floor in respect.

"Arise, Jedidiah. Sit beside me." He waved to a hovering servant. "Bring a chair for my son," David demanded hoarsely. The effort of speaking seemed almost to kill him as he fell back, chest heaving.

The scurrying servant returned soon with an ornate high-backed chair. Solomon moved it close enough to David's bed to allow him to hold his father's hand. It felt hot with fever.

"Ah, Jedidiah, it won't be long now," Israel's king whispered. "I feel the pull of death in my bones." His grasp was still strong as an ox. He loosened his grip and patted Solomon's hand.

"Father, I'm not ready for you to leave me," Solomon said, choking on the whispered words. He leaned over and touched his forehead to David's arm. "I'm not ready to be king. I am a grown man, but I feel I'm still a child, not a wise ruler as you are."

"Help me sit up, my son."

Solomon stood and grasped David under his arms. He lifted David, smaller and lighter than he used to be, and rearranged the cushions and pillows at his back. David relaxed against them with a groan. The sheen on his face and the feverish glow in his eyes revealed the inevitable.

Two servants approached and stood nearby to help if needed. David saw them and barked at them in irritation.

"Leave us!" He waited until they were gone before speaking.

"Jedidiah," he admonished, "one thing you must remember is to never show weakness or hesitation in the hearing of your servants. It doesn't matter how weak you feel—in their eyes you must be strong. Do you understand, my son?"

Solomon bowed his head. "Yes, Father, I understand."

"No one is ready to be king. If you bragged about being ready, you'd be the wrong choice. Your hesitation, your humility, both tell me you are surely God's man. In that regard, King Saul was right in his attitude. Early in his rule he began as God's humble servant. It was only later that he changed—"

David coughed hard, leaning forward until the fit passed. His cough was deep and violent, throwing blood-covered spittle over his chest and bedclothes. It had become worse over the last several weeks, and his physicians could not ease it.

Solomon turned his head away, unable to bear watching his strong father at the mercy of his illness. When the fit finally passed, he brought a cup of cold water to David's lips. He sucked at it greedily. Solomon wiped David's face with a damp cloth and cleaned away the reddish sputum from his chin.

"Thank you, Jedidiah. You're a good son. You will be a good king."

"There's no one like you, Father," Solomon murmured. "The One blesses your rule like no other king before you. I can't hope to govern his people as you."

David stared at Solomon for a moment, then closed his eyes. Solomon thought he'd gone to sleep as the moments passed. He slowly withdrew his hand from his father's, intending to slip away and let him rest, but David opened his eyes again. Solomon saw an unfamiliar shadow clouding his father's face.

"Father, what is it?"

David gripped Solomon's hand again with the fierceness of a father. Solomon covered David's hand gently and brought it to his lips.

"Father?"

"Do not compare yourself to me. Ever. I have disappointed God many times. Your mother…your brother…" He stopped midsentence, tears slipping down his cheeks. "It's only God's mercy that I'm still alive. It's only his mercy that will usher me to his side. And that same mercy will enable you to rule after me. He will show you what kind of ruler he would have you be. Do not try to copy me, my son, for then you will not be God's man—you will only be like me, a failure in many ways."

"Yes, Father. I will try to remember. Now please rest." Solomon didn't know whether his father's mortality or his regret was harder to bear.

David's eyes closed again. He still held Solomon's hand, and Solomon didn't want to remove it. The silence in the room was complete except for the buzz of an insect somewhere high in the chamber and the rasp of the king's breathing. Each inhale rattled loudly, and Solomon's heart broke with each labored breath.

You have never failed me, my king and my father.

After a time, Solomon relaxed against the chair cushions and allowed his heavy lids to close. His heart pulled him back in time. He recalled the stories he'd heard at his father's knee, warrior tales that never failed to enthrall the young boy. In Solomon's childish eyes, his father was a giant, almost godlike. His exploits made him famous to all Israel, but to Solomon it was more than fame—it was almost idol worship.

He used to sneak into his father's chamber and put his large leather war boots on his small feet and tramp around the room with a make-believe sword, slaying his own Goliaths. He'd loved sitting in front of his father on his warhorse as he inspected his troops, dreaming of the day when it would be his turn to strut in front of his men. But he never really thought it would be him—he had too many brothers vying for that honor.

He recalled stories of his father's three mighty men. How he'd dreamed as a youngster of following in their footsteps and making a name for himself. There was Jashobeam, who had killed eight hundred men with his spear in one battle. And Eleazar, who had stood with David against the entire Philistine army as the rest of their men fled. And Solomon's favorite—the story he'd asked for over and over—Shammah, who had defeated the Philistine army single handedly in, of all places, a field of lentils.

David and his mighty men had defeated the descendants of Goliath of Gath, including a huge man with six fingers on each hand and six toes on each foot.

The stories were so numerous he couldn't remember them all. But one of his favorites wasn't a war story at all. It took place when Solomon was a young man. His father had sinned against God by taking a census—motivated by kingly pride—and the nation was punished. After his repentance, God told David to go to the threshing floor of Araunah the Jebusite and build an altar there. David went and offered to buy the threshing floor, but Araunah wouldn't have any of that. He begged to give it to his king.

David had said, "No, I insist on buying it, for I will not present burnt offerings to the Lord my God that have cost me nothing."

That is my father, King David. I would be like him, Adonai. Let it be.

Solomon sighed. His father insisted it would be him sitting on the throne of Israel one day—God had told him—but Solomon just couldn't picture it. He no longer dreamed of going to war and slaying giants as his father had. Solomon dreamed of peace and prosperity. He knew the king had made detailed preparations to build a temple in Jerusalem, the place where God would dwell with his people. He knew his father would not be the one to build it—that honor would be his, Solomon's, God had decreed. And Solomon wanted to do just that. With all his heart he wanted to build the temple and lead his nation in worship of the one true God.

Make it so, Adonai. Make it so. I will be your true son if you place me on the throne of your people. I will obey you and lead your people in righteousness. I will give back to you the skill with the pen that you have given to me—I will honor you with my writing. Please give us peace and rest from war. I will follow you to the ends of the earth so that your name will be famous in all nations. But, Adonai, please remember I am but a child, innocent in the ways of the world. Help me to rule rightly and justly.

And Solomon slept with his hand in the king's and this prayer in his heart.

***

Many days later—Solomon lost count of the times he spent in the chair next to the king's deathbed—David lay dying. His council, joined by David's other sons, stood around his room, lining the walls out of respect for the king and his successor. The cough that had racked his frail body for so many weeks was gone. Solomon watched the gentle rise and fall of his chest.

He lightly touched his father's brow. The raging fever had finally broken, and his skin felt dry and cool. But it had taken its toll on the king who had ruled Israel for the last forty years, sapping his strength as impurities leached from precious metals.

What was left of the strong sovereign was small, weak, and dependent—and yet, somehow, he still emanated a powerful presence surely felt by every man in the room.

Solomon gently smoothed the thin straggly hair away from David's face, willing his father's eyes to open one more time. He got his wish.

"Jedidiah, is that you, my son? I can't see in this dim light," he said weakly.

"Yes, Father, I'm here. What do you wish?"

"Give me your hand, Jedidiah."

Solomon obeyed and laid his strong hand in his father's. David gripped it, trembling.

"I have something to say to you, my son, and I beg you to listen closely."

"Yes, my king and my father, I am listening."

"And not only listen. Hear and obey so that you will enjoy God's blessing and a long life."

"Yes, Father. Speak. I long to hear the instruction of such a wise and gentle king."

David snorted. "Gentle? No, I have been a warrior for my God. I have killed so many…so many men."

He seemed to drift off again. Solomon thought he was asleep, but he spoke again.

"It's you who will have a gentle reign." He shifted on his cushions, contriving to sit up straighter.

Solomon stood to help him, but the king waved him off.

"No," he said in a stronger voice. "Sit." He sounded now more like the king he was instead of a man close to death.

Solomon sat straight, both feet planted in front of him and his arms on the rests on either side of him.

I will now hear his last blessing. Adonai, please help him to say your words to me.

"Jedidiah, I am going where everyone on earth must someday go. Take courage and be a man. Observe the requirements of the Lord your God, and follow all his ways. Keep the decrees, commands, regulations, and laws written in the Law of Moses so that you will be successful in all you do and wherever you go. If you do this, then the Lord will keep the promise he made to me. He told me, 'If your descendants live as they should and follow me faithfully with all their heart and soul, one of them will always sit on the throne of Israel.'"

David paused a moment, love and desperation mingled on his ancient face.

"Jedidiah, do you understand? Do you commit to follow these instructions to your last breath?"

Solomon didn't have to think. It was exactly how he longed to live his life, with a passionate righteousness. He knew he'd never come close to being the king his father was, but with God's help he'd be the king God wanted him to be.

"Yes, Father, I do. With a willing heart and mind and all my strength, I will follow God and teach Israel to do so."

David nodded his head, satisfied with Solomon's fervent answer. He continued on, detailing other instructions to the next king of Israel, who sat before him.

***

The only sound was the scratching of the reed pen on papyrus and a cicada buzzing high above in the dimly lit room. The king favored this time of day for writing. His small private sanctuary was cut off from the late-afternoon noise in the main parts of his palace. Servants bustled about their duties preparing for the feasting tonight. He could hear the occasional laugh, the occasional argument, but he was not distracted. He was high above that normal life, solitary, listening to the One and scribing what he heard. The sun poured in from windows set high in the room, the only light. A small door opened to the balcony overlooking his palace courtyard. He liked to sit out there and watch the activity in the early morning, but today he'd slept late, plagued by aches and pains and the memories of years gone by.

He'd dreamed late into the morning, his life parading through the streets of his mind.

"The ark, the ark of God has returned to Jerusalem, the city of your father, David!" shouted the people in the courtyard in his dream. The procession of priests who had carefully brought the ark from its temporary shelter moved slowly up the steps of the temple, where they put it down in the exact place God had told King David to place it.

The dream changed.

The queen from the south, resplendent in her beauty, said to him on the last day of her sojourn in Israel, "Everything I heard in my country about your achievements and wisdom is true! How happy your people must be! Praise the Lord your God, who delights in you and has placed you on the throne of Israel. Because of the Lord's eternal love for Israel, he has made you king so you can rule with justice and righteousness." Sheba's queen then gave him many gifts, adding to his already overflowing treasury.

And the dream changed again, becoming a parade of beautiful women.

His wives, so many wives, each clamoring for his love and attention. He couldn't bring himself to turn any away—they were all so beautiful and intelligent. He wanted nothing more than to keep them happy. His dream became filled with them and their many gods—who now resided in shrines on every hilltop in Israel.

Remembering the dreams now, as he sat writing his poetry to Adonai, he was distracted. He stopped and laid his pen down, leaned forward, and rested his face in his hands.

What are you saying? Meaningless? Is that what you want me to say, Adonai? That all of life is meaningless?

No, my son. Only life without me is meaningless.

Ah, yes. As mine has been?

Silence. He didn't really expect an answer this time. Silence from the One said all that needed saying.

He groaned, recalling the women he'd had—over a thousand. The chariots and horses. The taxes collected, the slaves taken. His own palace the biggest, most luxurious in the known world. The respect and awe of the masses when taught by God-given wisdom. And the temple...the temple—erected according to God's plan to be his dwelling place.

He looked around the small room in which he spent most of his time now. This small room breathed Adonai's presence. Why had he ever thought he needed more than this? True, all that he had was lavished upon him by God—except the women. He'd taken foreign women and worshiped foreign gods to make his wives and concubines happy. He never could bear to disappoint a woman, and that weakness had turned his heart from God over and over again. King David's sin with his mother, Bathsheba, had been played out a thousandfold in his own life, almost making it seem insignificant by comparison. His worship of the one true God was sandwiched between that of Ashtoreth, Molech, Chemosh, and others. Recalling his spiritual degradation now was almost more than he could bear. How King David would despise him for it!

God had been angry with him and had told him the most devastating news that had ever reached a king's ears—his kingdom would be torn away and divided up. But because of David's faithfulness, God would hold back from ripping it away from Solomon during his lifetime. He would instead visit that judgment upon his son.

Oh, the misery of it! The grief that weighs me down! My hair has turned white with it. My feeble knees give way under it! I would die now and go to my place, if only I could.

But he could not lose hope—no, he could not. God had given him one more task to accomplish before he died, hence the hours and hours spent in this tiny room above his palace.

Solomon picked up the reed and began again.

"Everything is meaningless," says the Teacher, "completely meaningless!"

"I said to myself, 'Come on. Let's try pleasure. Let's look for the good things in life.' But I found that this, too, was meaningless."

"The more words you speak, the less they mean. So what good are they?"

"Live happily with the woman you love through all the meaningless days of life that God has given you under the sun. The wife God gives you is your reward for all your earthly toil."

"Whatever you do, do well. For when you go to the grave, there will be no work or planning or knowledge or wisdom."

"Light is sweet; how pleasant to see a new day dawning."

"Don't let the excitement of youth cause you to forget your Creator. Honor him in your youth before you grow old and say, 'Life is not pleasant anymore.'"

"Remember him…"

"Remember him…"

"Remember him…"

"Yes, remember your Creator now while you are young, before the silver cord of life

snaps and the golden bowl is broken. Don't wait until the water jar is smashed at the spring and the pulley is broken at the well. For then the dust will return to the earth, and the spirit will return to God who gave it."

"Everything is meaningless," says the Teacher, "completely meaningless."

"That's the whole story. Here now is my final conclusion: Fear God and obey his commands, for this is everyone's duty. God will judge us for everything we do, including every secret thing, whether good or bad."*

And the last king of undivided Israel sat in the dim light of the room, writing, writing, finally able to see where true meaning could be found. Not in wealth, not in women, not in prestige—but in passionate love for God and obedience to him.

Everything else was meaningless.

Today we might say that Solomon suffered from a severe case of clinical depression. He sounds almost suicidal. Today a psychologist would no doubt prescribe a complete array of counseling and antidepressants. Today he might be relegated to a psychiatric hospital until "cured."

But Solomon is obeying the Scriptures as he recalls how many times he left Adonai. The Bible tells us to mourn over our sins. Do we? Do we weep and wail? I think not. Most of the time when confronted with our spiritual infractions, we bow our heads (if even that), say a quick "Sorry, God," and go on our merry way.

Solomon, David's beloved Jedidiah, warns us to keep short accounts with our Creator—and start that practice while young. He lovingly reminds us that life is truly meaningless without God.

There was a time in my life when I left my Lover. I left him because life hadn't turned out the way I'd expected. I blamed him for not keeping his promises—to care for me, to give me work to do for him, to give me loving family relationships that would endure throughout eternity. I blamed him. Like an angry child, I stomped my feet, slammed the door in his face, and ran away. My heart was turned, as Solomon's, away from God in order to have what I wanted, what I thought I deserved.

When I came to my senses, largely because of harsh consequences he allowed me to suffer, I found an amazing thing. God had gone with me. He hadn't stayed behind the door I had slammed in his face. He was right behind me as I ran, and he protected me from harm I didn't know existed. I will always suffer some of those consequences, as will my family, because of my disobedience. The difference is, they will not destroy me, and through them I see his grace.

What turns your heart? Leaving the Lover of your soul is not reserved for the rich and famous—of any era. In every human heart there's a reserved space, put there by our Creator, for only him to occupy. Have you rented yours out to someone or something else? Perhaps it's time for you to open up that space, see who or what is roosting there, flash an eviction notice, and erect a *No Vacancy* sign.

What do you think? I'm getting the key to my space now…

Leaving Your Lover

Think About It...

For what sin in your past or your present have you refused to mourn? Mourning over any loss is hard work; how hard do you work at being grief-stricken over your own rebellion against the Lover of your soul?

Will you take the time now to name that rebellion—unadorned with modern, sugar-coated words that dilute the seriousness of sin—and kneel in today's version of sackcloth and ashes and ask God to help you see your sin exactly as he sees it?

*Selections from Ecclesiastes

Chapter 10
Whisper

And after the fire there was the sound of a gentle whisper.
~1 Kings 19:12

Elijah, his long dusty robes whipping about his feet, hurried along with his gray head pointed to the ground. His staff stabbed the dirt with each step. The sun overhead was merciless, the heat baking his neck and back. He adjusted his cloak to better cover his neck. He stopped for a moment, took the skin from around his waist, and swilled the water, letting it dribble down his chin and leak inside his tunic. He drained it, and his servant handed him another skin.

"How many do we have left, Elias?"

Elias opened his outer robe and displayed five more hanging around his waist.

"These five and that's all, Master."

"It's enough."

"Where are we going, Master, if I may ask?"

"You may, and I'll answer. We are going to see the king."

Elijah saw the younger man's face blanch white as new lamb's wool.

"Yes, Elias, we go to see Ahab and his snake of a wife. Their time is almost ended."

"Ended?" Elias squeaked. "What do you mean? Are you going to kill them?"

Elijah smiled wide, sun-burned cheeks bunching and eyes crinkling up.

"No, Elias. God will do that, I suspect. We go to give him a beginning."

With that, Elijah cinched up his outer robe and charged off at a faster pace than before, Elias running to keep up.

***

Jezebel paced. Back and forth she stormed in their private chamber, eyes blazing in anger. Ahab watched her carefully, unwilling to turn his back on her. Even though married to her, he didn't trust her when she was like this.

He recalled the time, many years ago, awakening from a sound sleep to see her standing over him in the dim light of the early morning. The long, curved blade of a dagger gleamed in her raised hand. He'd given her that dagger when they married, to offer her some protection from enemies. Now she pointed it at him! She was angry at some slight directed at her during an unruly gathering of peasants and had been disappointed in his handling of it. Before that day turned to night, the offender's head had been dangling from the city gate.

"Are you sure? He's coming here?" She stopped in front of him, hands on her hips. Her elaborately dressed hair and bejeweled fingers sparkled in the candlelight.

"Yes. Here."

"What does he want?"

"How should I know?"

"You should know. You're the king, or have you forgotten? Your spies are worthless!"

"That troubler of Israel will not live long, my sweet wife," he replied. "My worthless spies, as you call them, have a plan to dispose of him before he even reaches Samaria."

"Hmph! I'll believe that when I see it. And I'm not your 'sweet' wife. I'm your queen—and sometimes more of a king than you are. Remember that." She turned on her heel and stomped to the doorway.

"Give me news of his death this very day, or other heads will roll."

Left alone in the room, Ahab sighed and went to the windowed balcony overlooking the hill country. His father, Omri, had built this city on the hill, and now it was his to rule. The hill sloped down on all sides, making it an easily defensible fortress. No one could approach without being spotted by troops stationed around the perimeter and on top of the wall that ringed the city. Far south, in Judah, there was another king, and Ahab dreamed of the day when Israel would be one and he'd the king over all.

With Jezebel by my side, of course. Always with her by my side.

He remembered the day they'd met, like it was yesterday. She was but a sprite, her head barely reaching his chest. He'd seen her with her parents in a traveling caravan and had boldly approached her father to speak for her. When Jezebel realized what was happening, she'd thrust herself between the two men, eyes flashing and arms crossed in front of her.

"If you have something to say to me, sir, you will speak to me!" she'd demanded.

Ahab smiled at the memory of her father shrugging and stepping away from the two of them. By the end of that day, they were betrothed, and he bedded her to seal the bargain. He'd never regretted it—lack of trust notwithstanding.

Ahab was startled out of his musings by his aide entering to announce the new recruits were ready for inspection. *Recruits* was a misnomer. They had been ruthlessly snatched away from their families, boys still needing their mothers. But Ahab needed them more if he ever was to defeat that southern king. He donned his full dress armor, weapons at his waist, and went out. He would at least show them what a real soldier looked like.

Walking back and forth in front of the straggly group of thirty or so, Ahab had a hard time picturing them in battle. Some were no taller than his shoulder, and most were thin and scraggly. He stopped pacing and drew his sword. The boys nearest him shrank back, no doubt afraid the king was about to run them through. Instead, Ahab unexpectedly tossed it, grip first, to the nearest boy. The youngster grabbed at it but the weight was too much for him. It slipped from his one-handed grasp and clattered to the stone path at his feet. He looked up at the king with frantic eyes. He shrank to his knees, obviously trying to make himself even smaller than he was, hands in front of him to ward off a blow. Ahab started forward angrily but was held back by a hand on his arm. His aide moved between him and the boy.

"Sir, he'll learn. I promise you that. This one was found hiding in a well when we raided his village. I *will* pound bravery and discipline into him."

The king flung an arm in the boy's direction. "Look at him! He's shaking! And he needs some muscle on him. What can you do with him?"

"He's shaking because he's in the presence of a great king, my lord. How would you wish him to act in your presence?"

It was a crafty question, Ahab knew, designed to deflect his anger and flatter him at the same time.

Well, it's more than I get in my own home.

"All right. Take them and do your best. But I won't have them trembling in front of me. Better that they would stand tall if I have to run them through," he said, grinning. "And by the gods, feed them some good red meat. They'll need strength if they're to survive."

His aide nodded at him. "Yes, my king. The next time you see them, they'll be soldiers."

Ahab watched the boys herded through the courtyard to the outer gate. He knew they'd be forced to camp on the ground outside the city for at least a month, shepherded by his army's biggest and toughest soldiers—who wouldn't let them even relieve themselves without begging permission. He didn't envy them.

Leaving Your Lover

Ahab turned to go back into the palace, but a shout in the distance arrested his step. He shaded his eyes, looking outside the courtyard to the south. He saw, cresting the hill, a runner hell bent in his direction. He was alone, and the dust swirling up around his waist made him look like a small tornado.

Ahab waited just inside the gate. His aide had rejoined him.

"What do you think, sir? Bad news?"

"Runners rarely come with anything else."

The runner, his tattered sandals almost falling off his feet, pulled up short in front of them, bending over and coughing. Ahab waited patiently until he caught his breath. The man's tunic was ripped in several places and coated with a layer of sand. Flies buzzed about his head as he finally stood up straight, then dropped to one knee.

"Get up, man! What news?"

The man arose and pointed behind him. Ahab looked, one hand shading his eyes. He gasped and took a step backward. The man he'd just boasted to his wife would be killed before reaching Samaria walked steadily toward him. He had one servant in tow—no weapon, just a staff. Elijah lifted his gaze, and Ahab could see, even at this distance, that the prophet stared at him with eyes blazing. Ahab was curiously reminded of Jezebel's blazing eyes that very morning. Elijah stopped within spitting distance of him.

The old prophet threw his head covering back and stood motionless, his servant a respectful five paces behind. Ahab looked him up and down. For a moment neither of them spoke. The hot breeze blew across the sand, lifting the prophet's long, stringy hair from his neck. Somewhere in the mountains to the east a wild bird shrieked.

Ahab moved restlessly, his sword rattling at his side.

"So, false prophet, you don't kneel in the presence of your king?" Ahab knew Elijah wouldn't but thought he, the king, should address the infraction anyway. "I could have you killed for that," he added mildly.

Elijah ignored him. He placed one foot in front of the other, hunching forward, with one long, claw-like finger pointed at Ahab.

"As surely as the Lord, the God of Israel, lives—the God I serve and the only one I kneel to—there will be no dew or rain during the next few years until I give the word!"

Elijah cried the words with a fierceness that made Ahab's skin crawl.

Then it was over. Before Ahab could react, Elijah and his servant pivoted swiftly and strode back the way they'd come. Ahab didn't move until they reached the crest of the hill and disappeared over the edge.

"Of all the impudent brashness! As if *he* controls the rain!"

"My lord, does he know whom he has to deal with?" his aide asked.

"Who are you talking about? Ba`al or Jezebel?"

"Both," his aide replied with a mischievous grin.

Ahab could now just barely make out the two tiny forms against the desert floor in the distance.

"No, I don't think he does. He's just thrown down the gauntlet to the rain god and to that god's priestess. It doesn't bode well for him, eh? Come on. I'd best go confess to both of them that we've let him slip through our fingers again."

Ahab looked up at a particular window high in the palace wall. "Perhaps it'll be our heads on the gate by nightfall."

***

Some thirty months later, Ahab stood at his private balcony gazing out over the parched land. He'd just returned from an extensive search throughout the land for any sign of spring or vegetation that would save his mules and horses. He'd found nothing.

The drought the prophet had predicted was in its third year and showed no signs of ending. He went daily to the shrines and offered sacrifices, but the rain god Ba`al was silent. The instigator of this famine had disappeared into thin air. Jezebel had not forgiven her husband yet—she wouldn't even let him near her. He was forced to find relief with other more disreputable women. He bowed his head, fists tightening at his sides in frustration.

What does she expect me to do? Take my army and search for him? In this drought, we wouldn't last a day out there.

He shook his head, turning as his aide appeared in the doorway.

Briefly dropping to one knee, then standing, his aide approached.

"Sire, I have news," he whispered.

"Don't whisper! We're quite alone, you know," Ahab replied loudly.

His aide stepped back.

"You know she hasn't graced this room in months. So what news?"

His aide looked uncomfortable. "Yes, my lord. The news is this: Elijah is on his way here."

"What? Again? You have this on good authority?"

"Yes. Obadiah is without. He brings you this news."

"Obadiah? What has my chief steward to do with this? I sent him to look for water and food weeks ago, not to seek out some worthless prophet!"

His aide remained silent, waiting until Ahab's anger subsided.

"Well? What do you say? Don't keep me in suspense. Did he find nothing except this dried-up false prophet?"

"Yes, he has just returned, and he found nothing. As to the other, I'll let him tell you."

The aide stepped to the doorway and beckoned. Obadiah, trembling from head to foot, approached Ahab and dropped to his face. The poor man hadn't even been allowed to wash and gulp some water before being dragged here before him—the stench was overpowering.

"Oh, get up, you miserable follower of a false god. Get up, or I'll call Jezebel and have her deal with you. Would you like that? I'm sure she'd be interested to know about those one hundred false prophets who languished in caves under your tender care."

Obadiah blanched. "No, my lord, please." He immediately arose and stood silent before Ahab with eyes downcast.

"So I take it you found no water or grass?"

"No, my lord." He finally looked Ahab in the eye. "But I found Elijah, my lord. Or rather, he found me. And he is here. To see you."

Ahab was silent, nostrils flared, eyes narrowed. Obadiah stepped back, eyes darting, as if to find a place to hide.

Ahab looked him up and down with disdain. "Go back to your duties," he growled. "And wash before you come to me again!"

Obadiah scuttled away.

Ahab retrieved his sword and armor from an alcove and swiftly put them on.

"Let's go see this 'prophet,' as he calls himself." Ahab led the way out, his aide close behind.

Elijah stood erect in the gate, in the same spot he'd stood three years earlier, looking even older and more bedraggled. His servant stood behind him and to his left. Ahab couldn't help but be aware of the power emanating from the old prophet. In spite of his age and desert-beaten appearance, his eyes were fierce, mouth set firmly in a thin line, his demeanor giving no appearance of weakness. As before, he carried no weapon, just his thick staff, which reached at least a yard above his head. The breeze whipped his tattered robes around him. His eyes never left Ahab's.

Ahab stepped to within inches of Elijah, sword rattling at his side. He intended to make the old man nervous, but he might as well have tried to make a boulder flinch. Elijah didn't move, so Ahab had to give up and take a step back.

"So. Is it really you, you troublemaker of Israel?"

The prophet's servant moved suddenly, stepping to Elijah's side. Ahab's hand grasped his sword hilt.

"Stay, my good man, or you'll be in the presence of your fictitious god before your next breath," he cautioned.

Elijah gripped his man's arm and gently pushed him back to a position behind him.

"I have made no trouble for Israel," he said. "You and your family are the troublemakers, for you have refused to obey the commands of the Lord and have worshiped the images of Ba`al instead. Now summon all Israel to join me at Mount Carmel, along with the four hundred and fifty prophets of Ba`al and the four hundred prophets of Asherah, who are supported by Jezebel."

Just as before, Elijah delivered his ultimatum and left before Ahab could even formulate a response. He watched, as before, the prophet, with his servant in tow, make his way to the crest of the hill and disappear below.

"What will we do, my lord?" asked his aide.

Ahab stood still, thinking. An insect buzzed incessantly near his right ear, and he swatted it. He turned and looked back at his palace, to that window high on the south side. He thought he detected movement.

"Why, we will do as he said," he replied calmly. "We'll have a showdown. Let's go tell my esteemed wife."

***

Elijah sat under his solitary broom tree as the sun sank into the western desert. He was wasted, having charged from Mount Carmel to Jezreel, then to Beersheba, where he'd left Elias. He'd traveled all day and knew he couldn't go any farther. He hardly knew where he was going anyway. An idea had lodged in his mind earlier—go to the Mountain of Yahweh—but he'd never make it that far. The thought of traveling another two hundred miles in this hellhole of a desert was unthinkable.

So now what? Am I to turn to dust under this tree?

Elijah shook his head. He'd defeated the 850 false prophets owned by Jezebel. They had been her power base—she'd bought and paid for them, and their sole job was to deify herself and Ahab and help perpetuate their kingdom. The God of Israel had made short work of them. Mount Carmel would forever be known as the place where the Ba`als and Yahweh had come head to head in an astounding fireball from heaven. And not only that. The rain had finally come—after three years of drought—almost immediately after the prophets of Ba`al were turned to ash. The fierce downpour had washed away all trace of Jezebel's prophets, their ashes sliding down the mountainside and disappearing in the streams as if they'd never been.

To say Jezebel is angry is a serious understatement.

Jezebel's message replayed itself in his mind. *May the gods strike me and even kill me if by this time tomorrow I have not killed you just as you killed them.* Coming from Ahab's queen, it was no idle threat, so he'd run as far and as fast as he could.

He turned red-rimmed eyes to the horizon. The sun was almost down now, but the heat remained. As far as he could see, there was nothing but sand and the occasional scrub tree, like the one under which he'd collapsed. He had only two skins of water and no food. He was completely alone, unless he counted the wind scorpion that had appeared out of nowhere to rest in the shade of his right foot. They eyed each other for a moment. Elijah jerked his foot, and the creature sped off, churning up the desert like a tiny sand storm.

Why did I run from her? She flicked her feeble finger at me, and like the wind scorpion, I've churned up the desert to get away. The God of Israel killed her prophets. Would he not have saved me from her?

Elijah bowed his weary head, shoulders heaving. *Adonai, why did I run? She's no match for you. I've failed you.*

He slumped to his side in the sand as the sun finally dipped below the horizon, bringing a cool wind.

I have had enough, Lord. Take my life, for I am no better than my ancestors who have already died.

Elijah slept. The moon rose over the desert, shining on the exhausted prophet of Israel's God.

Get up and eat!

Elijah awoke with a start. He'd felt the touch of a hand in his sleep and now heard this voice. He looked to his right and saw some baked bread and a jar of water arranged on a flat rock.

Father?

Elijah ate and drank and lay back down, immediately falling into a deep sleep.

Get up and eat some more, or the journey ahead will be too much for you.

Journey? Journey to where, Adonai?

There was no answer. Elijah got up and ate and drank his fill. After he'd eaten, he stood for a moment, gazing south.

The Mountain of Yahweh. Yes, Adonai.

Elijah girded his tunic around him, settled his head covering, and picked up his staff.

I'll probably die before I get there, but at least I'll die going in the right direction.

Forty days and forty nights later, sustained by food and water God had provided, he came to a cave on Mount Horeb, where he would shelter for the night. As soon as he'd arrived, the strength God had given him leaked away. He spread his outer tunic on the moist sand inside the cave and lay down to sleep. He was out cold in just a few seconds.

What are you doing here, Elijah?

Elijah bolted up. He had no idea how long he'd slept, but he felt refreshed.

"I have zealously served the Lord God Almighty. But the people of Israel have broken their covenant with you, torn down your altars, and killed every one of your prophets. I am the only one left, and now they are trying to kill me too."

To his own ears, it sounded like a litany of whining, but at least he was honest. Elijah sat on the hard ground, waiting for God to answer or strike him dead.

I don't really care which.

Go out and stand before me on the mountain.

"Yes, Lord."

Elijah wrapped his cloak around him and stepped outside the cave.

Now I will speak face to face with Adonai.

But as soon as Elijah's feet touched the sand outside the cave, a mighty windstorm struck the mountain. The sudden fierce gale threatened to rip his outer tunic and head wrap from his body. Small rocks dislodged from above and rained down as Elijah flattened himself against the stone to the right of the cave entrance.

Adonai?

No answer.

The wind diminished as suddenly as it had begun. He ventured to the edge of the cliff face and looked down. Small trees, scrubs, and large rocks had been picked up by the wind and deposited haphazardly on the path leading down the mountain. He looked closely at one boulder and saw the legs of a lion protruding from under it. He backed from the ledge on shaky legs.

Just as he gained the cave entrance, the entire mountain rocked.

Oh, God, now an earthquake?

Boulders from above now rolled down, and the ground beneath Elijah's feet split just as he jumped back.

Yahweh! Save me!

No answer.

As the earthquake subsided, the scrub brush around the cave surged with fire, as if a hot blast from above had ignited them. Elijah stared down the slope and out into the plain—everywhere he looked fires burned. Not only the mountain, but the desert beyond and even the sand blazed with fire. He shrank back from the sizzle. He felt the heat down to his toes and looked down. The hem of his robe smoked and turned black, tiny flames visible.

Elijah beat the flames out. He retreated, quaking, inside the cave entrance.

Lord! Where are you?

No answer.

As he stared out at the inferno, the raging fires suddenly blinked out as if they'd never been. Shocked, Elijah was at the end of his tether. Now the air was filled with thick, heavy smoke. The stench of it crowded his throat and burned his eyes. He felt his mind give way as he dropped to his knees inside the cave and pleaded silently for God to kill him and be done with it.

Lord, what are you doing? Just take me now, please!

No answer.

Elijah tried to quiet his heart, tried to pray, but terror swallowed his effort.

Then, ever so gently, a tender breeze drifted into the cave. It lifted the smoke away, surrounding Elijah with a delicious aroma—and with it something else, barely discernible above the frightful cacophony in his mind.

A whisper? Or was it? Who could it be?

Elijah arose, wrapped his cloak around him, and put one unsteady foot outside the cave and leaned out, straining to hear. A voice floated to him on the breeze. At least he thought it was a voice. What was it saying? Elijah now had both feet outside the cave. He looked this way and that, trying to see the body attached to the voice. As the smoke floated away, he saw no one nearby.

What are you doing here, Elijah?

Adonai? Don't you know why I'm here? You told me to come here.

He repeated himself, "I have zealously served the Lord God Almighty. But the people of Israel have broken their covenant with you, torn down your altars, and killed every one of your prophets. I am the only one left, and now they are trying to kill me too."

Adonai did not answer him. Elijah's shoulders drooped. Confusion mounted as he stood on the Mountain of God waiting for answers.

And then, finally, in the gentlest of whispered words, God told Elijah what he needed to hear most.

Do you now stand on your mountain waiting for answers? Are you afraid of your present situation? Are you running from them? Have you found, as Elijah did, that you cannot outrun your overwhelming circumstances? Do you seek God, as Elijah did, in all the wrong places?

God was not in the windstorm, the fire, nor the earthquake. Elijah had to quiet his heart, calm his mind, and strain to hear God's whisper. He had to plow through the confusion of his predicament and push it aside to get to God. And when he was finally there, God gave him the message he needed to hear—clear instructions and a final encouraging word.

Yet I will preserve seven thousand others in Israel who have never bowed down to Ba`al or kissed him!

Do you sometimes feel as Elijah did, that you alone in your home, your workplace, your school, your community are the only one who trusts God and obeys him? Do you feel as if you are always swimming against the tide and never reaching the shore? You're tired and want to give up. You want to be able to talk to coworkers and family members without confrontation. You'd even like to be able to turn on the evening news and not hear about mass shootings, the latest perversion in Hollywood, or the new scandal in our nation's capital. You feel isolated, contending for holiness in a polluted world.

But there's hope. The same words spoken to Elijah on his mountain are declared to you today. There are followers of Yeshua on every continent, in every nation, on every street the world over. We are not alone.

And Elijah teaches us that when we feel most alone in the world, that is when God is most with us. Lean forward and listen. He's whispering to you now.

What circumstances have led you to this mountain where you seek the One you've been unable to find? Do you feel alone in your struggle to make sense of what has happened to you?

Will you strain to hear what God is saying to you in a whisper—that you are not alone, that he is there beside you, and that he will send help to you as soon as you stop your struggle and lean in close and tight with him?

Chapter 11
Swallowed

But Jonah got up and went in the opposite direction to get away from the Lord.
~Jonah 1:3

The prophet bolted up from his mat. His robes clung to him in damp folds. His muscles ached as if he'd wrestled an enemy in his sleep.

The dream! The dream again!

He looked out the window of his small rooftop room in Gath-hepher. The moon still hung small and cold in the black sky. He arose and stared at the night, judging it to be about two hours before dawn.

He'd come home to visit his family. His mother, his cousins, and his one sister had welcomed him with open arms and listened spellbound to tales of his adventures. He'd relaxed, eaten good home cooking, and had gone to bed that first night believing the dream would not visit him again. He'd been wrong, so wrong. It'd been four days, and the dream had plagued him every night. It was wearing him down. He wasn't sleeping well. Even his sister asked him what was wrong.

"Jonah, you're looking so haggard," she'd said. "What's bothering you?"

He'd given her some vague answer. How could he tell his family about the dream? They'd conclude he was unhinged.

Maybe he was crazy. Maybe his mind was going. Maybe he should just ignore it. Maybe if he ignored it, it would just stop. Maybe.

Maybe I ate some bad food a week ago and that's why I'm beset by these thoughts. Yes, that must be it. Some more of Mother's cooking—and some rest—will put everything right.

Jonah knelt and prayed, as was his usual morning ritual, asking God to direct him. It felt empty, but still Jonah resisted the urge to give it up. Maybe God would hear him this time.

Jonah turned from the window, changed into his day clothes, and made his way down the rooftop stairs. Entering through the open kitchen doorway, he smelled his mother's flat cakes and rice. The table was laid with simple plates and cups. He shooed a goat away from the doorway and gave his sister a kiss on the cheek.

"You look better this morning, brother. Did you sleep well?"

"Yes," he lied. "Didn't wake up once." That much was true. He hadn't awakened from the dream, but his body ached with fatigue and his thoughts circled like buzzards over a carcass.

His mother turned from the table and stared at him with narrowed eyes.

"My son, I suckled you at my breast, kissed away your bruises, was there when you were raised from the dead by the man of God, and believed you when you announced you were chosen by God to be his prophet. And now you stand here and lie to my face in my own home. Something *is* wrong. Tell me." Her old voice was still strong and brooked no dissent.

The two women faced him side by side like a tribunal pronouncing a death sentence.

Jonah shifted uncomfortably, hands hanging loose at his sides. His eyes could not, would not meet his mother's. He heard the call of a wild animal through the open doorway, then the scream of its prey.

Leaving Your Lover

How can I tell them? It's the most bizarre dream ever dreamed—if I do what the man tells me, my life will surely end in the most gruesome way.

He winced just thinking about the violent stories he'd heard—Assyria was well known for inventing new ways to torture her enemies before finishing them off. He'd once heard of a man who'd been captured by Assyrian soldiers and made to hang upside down on a stake each night as they traveled back to their camp. And each night, a soldier came and cut a small piece from him—a finger, a toe, an ear, a slice of skin—until when they arrived at their destination, there wasn't much left of him. But he'd lived to tell about it.

If I go there, it'll be all over for me and for them. They will be alone. No, I can't do it. And they must never know.

"Mother, I'm tired. That's all." He moved to her side and took her wrinkled hand into his strong one. "My body is tired and my mind is tired. I've been sleeping on the ground for weeks. I've been eating my own cooking—hardly the good fare I find here at your table—and I've announced judgment to people who point and stare at me as if I'm crazy. I give God's message over and over again, and hardly anyone listens. Do you know what that feels like? I just need to rest a few days before I leave again. I need to spend time with my family and friends—to reconnect with those who really care about me."

"Mother, he's right," his sister said quietly, stepping forward and reaching for his other hand. "Let's let him be and share a meal. Let's laugh together, catch him up on all the town gossip, and listen to more of his stories. It's what my brother needs."

His mother searched his face and nodded slowly. "All right. I'll stop hounding you—for now. And there *are* some chores that need a man's attention." She turned away from him, shoulders set. "Well," she said briskly, "sit down. The food is getting cold."

***

A week later he fled frantically for Joppa.

He'd stayed a few more days with his mother, enduring her insistent interrogations. When he accompanied his sister to the small market in the center of Gath-hepher, neighbors he'd grown up with stared at him and whispered, heads shaking and fingers pointing. Word had gotten round that there was something off about Jonah, son of Amittai.

That very afternoon he'd had his first waking dream—a vision in broad daylight as he rested in his rooftop room. A dream more vivid than any night hallucination he'd experienced.

A man, glowing and indistinct, with hair and beard of fire and a staff with a snake's head atop it, appeared outside his open window, then walked on air through the window and sat on his mat. Jonah lay frozen, unable to move or think. The man spoke. His voice sounded like a great torrent of water rushing over a rocky cliff.

"Get up and go to the great city of Nineveh. Announce my judgment against it because I have seen how wicked its people are."

The man then stood and walked out the window, becoming smaller to fit through it, then becoming larger than he'd been while in the room. Jonah sprang up and leaped to the window. He could still see the man, his massive feet walking over the world, stepping on the mountaintops, then disappearing into the sunlit distance. Jonah stood frozen at the window for a long time as he tried to make sense of what he'd just seen.

Jonah had shaken himself and determined then and there he must leave Gath-hepher immediately. He'd gotten his things together the next day, said goodbye to his family and friends, and left the town in the dust. His mother had kissed his brow and told him to take care of himself. When she'd asked where he was going, he told her not to worry.

"I'm going where God has told me to go," he'd lied.

He headed southwest, not northeast—the exact opposite direction from Nineveh. As he rapidly put his hometown behind him, he allowed his mind to review the dreams. He scrutinized every detail of every one, finally deciding they were nothing more than the creations of a dissatisfied life. Really! A man squeezing through a small window and then disappearing the same way? Was this a traveling prophet's hazard—a deranged mind? He didn't really like traveling, and he certainly hadn't liked pronouncing judgment on scores of people who hadn't cared a fig for his words. Now God wanted him to go to Assyria, where they probably wouldn't care for his words either. But they wouldn't just throw melons at him. In his mind's eye he saw that poor man on the pole...

The strain of it is finally catching up with me.

After several miles, his mind was settled. He need pay no more attention to these dreams than he did a fly buzzing around his head. Maybe he'd take up another trade. He liked to fish when he got the chance. Perhaps when he reached the bustling seaport of Joppa, he would inquire into the possibility of joining a crew and earning some real money instead of the paltry offerings a prophet received—baskets of moldering figs and fish and the occasional coin.

Jonah now felt more optimistic than he had in weeks, his confidence building with each step. As he walked down the dusty road to Joppa, he imagined the next time he'd visit his mother, bringing with him fistfuls of coin to give her, earned as a fisherman.

As he thought of that pleasant possibility, guilt rose in his chest. He'd lied to his mother. Would she even be pleased at the wealth he'd someday share with her? He pushed the thought down into that hidden place.

I'll think on it no longer. Surely God does not expect me to risk my life in such a brutal place as Assyria. Surely he wants me to be happy and successful in order to help my family.

Yes! I'll be a success at this. I know I will.

He had a sudden thought, rising to the foreground of his mind. He wasn't a very successful prophet, by all accounts, so he'd better petition God about his new direction. Couldn't hurt.

God, please help me be a success at this.

***

Four days and sixty miles later, the port of Joppa lay before Jonah's eyes. It was a busy place, especially at the shore where Jonah now stood. Fishing boats were everywhere, their catches laid out in shining bundles along the beach. Captains shouted their prices and merchants waved their hands to buy. It was an exhilarating scene.

Jonah made his way through the throng, taking in the coin changing hands, the fresh sea breeze, and the children running in and out among their parents. He took a deep breath. He had had no dreams or visions during the days on the road. He'd slept soundly each night and had awoken refreshed.

Surely God is pleased with me. I've rejected those awful dreams—certainly not given by him but by some demon to get me off track. Why else would they have stopped?

Jonah comforted himself with these thoughts. He sat down on a rock at the edge of the water to plan his next move. He watched the boats coming and going, looking for one large enough to need another man. He saw one now, sliding into port. He shaded his eyes and watched the men disembark, hauling their nets behind them. He thought they looked a decent crew. And one seemed to be injured, limping, supported by two other crew members. They laid him on the beach. One of the men bent down and exposed a great bloody gash ripped open on the man's thigh.

Perhaps...

His thoughts were interrupted by a young boy suddenly appearing in front of him, blocking his view. He looked like a street urchin, unkempt and dirty. He stood silent, staring at Jonah. The shouting of the crowds around them faded from Jonah's hearing. The beach slowly disappeared as if blown away by the sea breezes. All Jonah could see was the boy, and all he could hear was his own heartbeat.

"Who are you, and what do you—"

"Why are you here, man of God?" the boy shrieked, loud enough to wake the dead. "Why aren't you in Nineveh?"

Jonah frantically looked around. He stood and gripped the boy by the neck of his filthy tunic, lifting him to eye level. The boy's feet dangled ten inches from the ground. He didn't struggle.

"What are you talking about, boy? Who are you?"

And then the boy was gone. Simply gone. Jonah's hands now gripped nothing but air. He sat down hard on his rock, fighting for breath. The busy port noises returned—merchants hawking their wares, children playing. The scene switched back on as if it had never left.

But now something else. The shouting throng quieted, every face pointed his way, as if they were the audience and he on a stage. Their faces were indistinct, except for their mouths. Each pair of lips whispered only one word, becoming louder, insistent with each repetition.

Nineveh.

Nineveh.

Nineveh.

Over and over again he heard the word—murmured, hissed, muttered. Every direction he looked, even out to sea, where disembodied heads hovered over the waves, the blank faces crowded his vision, mouths beating out the same word.

Nineveh.

His heart threatened to burst from his chest with each terrified beat. He gripped his hair and pulled hard, hoping the pain would clear his mind and his vision. He squeezed his eyes shut, then opened them again.

Ah! Normal again. The boats drifted in and out of the harbor, children laughing, tradesmen shouting. Jonah stood and made his way on shaky legs to the captain of the boat that had just put in. He stood over his injured man, listening to the report of his condition.

"Sir, do you have room for another hand?"

"No," answered the captain, eyes raking Jonah. "I just hired that fellow over there," he said, pointing to a giant of a man. "I need a real crew member, not some phony desert prophet."

Jonah desperately dug into his money bag.

"Then can I pay you to take me where you are going?"

The captain's eyes gleamed at the coin in Jonah's hand.

"Yes, of course. You'll have to sleep rough though."

"No matter."

Jonah handed over the coin. "Where *are* you going, sir?"

"West, to Tarshish."

Jonah nodded.

Southern Spain? Good. Hundreds of miles away from Nineveh. I'll start a new life. Nothing can hinder me now. Perhaps along the way this captain will hire me on as one of the crew. Maybe in the galley, if I prove useful.

Jonah walked the plank into the boat and stood at the rail, looking west.

Yes, a new life. Away from Assyria, away from Nineveh.

***

Jonah awoke from a nightmare. He felt caught, strapped, unable to move for the fear that had overtaken him.

The Assyrians had captured him, stripped him naked, and threw him into an abandoned well, moist and slimy with mold. The smell gagged him. He was lying on a pile of putrefied garbage.

He opened his eyes but saw nothing. He touched the decaying garbage, his hands sinking into the slime with each movement. Now he felt something, a solid shape. Running his fingers over the shape, he was terrified to realize it was a human skull. He jerked his hand back.

He strained to see, but the blackness was complete. This dream was far worse than any other. It seemed so real. A thought drifted lazily across his dream world, and Jonah knew the truth.

Real because it was real.
What?

Jonah, shocked to his very core, abruptly knew he was awake, not dreaming. The nightmare was real. It had followed him into consciousness, was around him, touching him, swallowing him.

Where am I?

He remembered he had been captured by the Assyrians, but—

I don't remember being with them. I don't remember the capture. All I remember is getting on a boat and sailing to Tarshish. And I remember...

Now it came back to him, but in small chunks. The storm. The sailors beseeching their gods to save them. The lottery. The realization he was to blame for the storm. Telling the men to toss him into the sea. The splash. Sinking into oblivion. The dim outline far below him of a great creature swimming lazily toward him. It reached him, turned sideways, and slid past him, its enormous eye scanning him inches from his face, his bare belly raked bloody by its rough scales. Then the monster swam down and out of sight.

Thank you, God!

Sinking, sinking, his lungs bursting in his chest. Then a great mouth, outlined by small gleaming teeth, appeared below him, opening, sucking him in. After that, he remembered nothing until this moment.

This is no garbage-filled well. This is the inside of the creature. It swallowed me! Oh, God, what have I done? No one has ever been so unlucky!

Jonah kicked his feet to raise his shoulders above the digesting food, but the effort only caused him to sink farther into the soft, slimy folds. He panicked. He tried to push himself up with his hands, but soon he was chest deep. The stench was overpowering. He vomited, adding to his misery.

Jonah finally gave up struggling and hung there, his feet touching nothing underneath him, his arms suspended out to his sides as if floating in a pool. The least movement caused him to sink, so he stilled himself. He could do nothing for himself except think.

***

And think he did—for three days and three nights. And when he was done thinking, he gave up another struggle. He prayed to God from inside the sea creature, acknowledging his disobedience to the one who'd arranged his present predicament.

Then, terror of terrors, the beast grunted and belched. Jonah's head was suddenly under the slime. He tried to push up, but there was nothing to push up against. He choked, he vomited again, sucking in some of the slime. So this was to be his punishment, to suffocate and die inside this filthy, slimy cave in the middle of the sea. Jonah could feel the sway of the giant fish, like ocean waves rising and falling. He waited for death to come. But it didn't.

The great fish, with a final watery groan, pushed Jonah up and out of his gut along with a goodly amount of his stomach contents. Jonah lay on a beach, covered with slime. He was no longer God's much-loved prophet. He was just regurgitated garbage deposited on a deserted shore. He opened one eye to see the great fin skimming the water and disappearing once again into the deep.

He rolled over, wiping the rotting slime from his eyes and nose. The smell made him vomit again. He managed to get to his feet and plunge under the waves, washing himself as best he could. When he came up out of the water, he heard the call of a bird high in the sky. The bird flew low over his head and turned one eye downward to meet Jonah's, then flapped off in the opposite direction. Toward Nineveh.

Jonah knelt there in the water and gave up his struggle again. He would go where God commanded, and if he was slain, however gruesomely, at least he would obey.

Jonah then went to Nineveh, preached God's message—and to his dismay, the Ninevites repented of their wickedness. He hated the Assyrians and didn't want them to repent and be blessed by God. He wanted God to destroy them for their evil ways. They deserved nothing from God but retribution. His story ends with him sitting under a leafy plant overlooking the great city. As he sat and nursed his grudge, God caused a worm to gnaw on the leafy plant, destroying it and the shade it had afforded Jonah. His misery knew no bounds.

And God chastised him for his hatred of the worm and the Assyrians, making it clear to *us* that that there is no person or people group outside the bounds of his control. He will love whom he loves, and we'd best fall in line with his plans.

Centuries later, another of God's servants went to Joppa. Simon Peter's story is similar to Jonah's. They were both called to preach to Gentiles—Jonah in Assyria, Peter to the Gentiles living around him. To both, it was a radical move in their day, to preach repentance and salvation to a people whom Jews felt were inferior to them.

There are, however, significant differences between their stories. Peter was in Joppa because God sent him there. Jonah was in Joppa because he was running from God. Peter chose to obey God's call, risking severe criticism from other believers. Jonah had to be convinced, in the worst way, to go where God called him and preach to the people to whom God had called him.

Jonah learned the hard way that God directs every creature in the universe and they are at his disposal to use as he sees fit. He can even use whales and worms and birds to accomplish his plans.

May we not abandon ourselves, as Jonah did, to our prejudices, our grudges, and our hatreds. May we realize that the God who loves us loves all.

We will never know the outcome of our obedience unless we obey.

Leaving Your Lover

Think About It...

Has your rebellion toward God swallowed you whole, leaving you no wiggle room, no way out? Are you now surrounded by rotting garbage, those heartrending consequences produced by your rebellion? Will you give up and repent?

Are you afraid of the consequences if you now repent and obey God? Will you let God be God and handle those consequences?

Chapter 12
The Kiss

*So Judas came straight to Jesus. "Greetings, Rabbi!" he
exclaimed and gave him a kiss.*
~Matthew 26:49

"Judas! How are you this fine morning?"

Swiftly turning to see who hailed him, Judas of Kerioth saw his childhood friend Lieber running to catch up with him. He stopped and waited. The morning sun was just breaking over the mountain. It was going to be a hot day.

Out of breath, Lieber halted in front of him, hair dark and beard wild, and clapped him on the shoulder. Judas waited until his comrade had enough breath to speak.

"I'm fine. Quite a crowd, hmm?" Judas's eyes roamed over the hillside. Scores of people climbed with them, all heading to the knoll just above where they stood.

Lieber nodded. "What do you think he wants, my friend? Do you think it's finally going to happen? My father says it's about time."

Judas glanced around. "Where is your father?"

"He's too ill to come. He sent me in his stead," Lieber replied, drawing himself up proudly.

"I'm sorry to hear he's ill," Judas replied politely, his attention now diverted by the teacher's strong voice calling from above.

The two men started climbing again and were soon standing on the fringe of the mass of disciples. Judas judged there were at least fifty in the crowd, grouped in front of a small rise where the teacher stood slightly above them.

Lieber leaned over and whispered, "Did you hear his voice in your sleep like I did? I thought it was a dream until I woke up and realized I could still hear him. At first I was scared. Then I knew who it was. He called me to come here this morning. Was it like that for you?"

Judas studied his friend's face. They'd known each other since they were youngsters, and they had been fast friends since the day Lieber had taken the blame for his own thievery in the Kerioth market. They were both seven years old at the time. Judas had tried to hide a small bunch of grapes in his tunic and dropped them and had been caught. Lieber told the fruit seller he'd done it and had borne the cuffing from the angry man. When Lieber's parents found out, he'd been banished to the sheep pen for a month. Judas tried always to be kind to his friend because of loyalty, but he was tediously plodding at times and a slow thinker.

"No, I wasn't sleeping when I heard him. I was trying to kiss Abra behind the tanner's shop." Judas smiled at the memory.

"You weren't, my friend! If her father finds out, he'll beat you."

"Shh! Keep your voice down. He won't find out. She won't say anything. Anyway, it didn't happen. She pushed me down and ran. But it will happen someday." He stopped and looked Lieber in the eye. "I will marry her one day. You'll see."

"But what about the teacher's call? Were you really…"

"After Abra ran away, I picked myself up out of the dirt, and then his voice was in my ear or my head, not sure which. He bid me come to the mountain today. So here I am. I wonder what he wants."

They now found themselves pushed into the center of the throng as more disciples crowded onto the small knoll. The sun had climbed over their heads, and the slight breeze stilled. It was stifling where Judas and Lieber stood, hemmed in on all sides. Judas put his sleeve to his nose against the smell of unwashed bodies.

Jesus finally seemed satisfied that everyone was here and spoke loudly.

"We will pray now." He bowed his head, and instantly all followed suit.

"My Father in heaven, you have given me these. May I rightly decide whom you have named to be your apostles."

Apostles? I wonder what that means...

Jesus raised his head and called out names. As he did so, those he named stepped through the mass of people and stood next to him.

"Simon!"

Simon threw a shocked look at his brother Andrew and stumbled forward and fell to his knees in front of Jesus of Nazareth. Judas could see Andrew's face working. He couldn't stem the tide of tears.

"Andrew!"

Andrew pushed his way through the crowd and locked arms with Simon.

As the sun rose higher in the sky, Jesus called name after name until there were eleven men ranged out on either side of him. Each man had looked shocked and confused when his name was called. Each one had come forward and knelt before Jesus. Each one had risen and been drawn into a loving embrace with Jesus. Jesus had whispered into each man's ear. Judas wondered what Jesus whispered to them to cause their confusion to give way to such joy. Their faces shone like the sun.

Simon Peter, Andrew, James, John, Philip, Bartholomew, Matthew—*Levi, the tax collector?*—and his brother James, Thomas, Simon the Zealot, and Jude all stood on either side of Jesus arm in arm. Judas of Kerioth knew them all, and he wondered what was next. Would they teach with the teacher? Would they travel with him? What about their families?

Judas was jerked out of his thoughts by a sudden hiss. He looked up and locked eyes with the man in front of him, who had turned toward him, hands on hips. Then he saw that everyone was watching him and waiting for something.

"What? What happened?"

They broke into loud guffaws. Those closest to him clapped him on the back.

"Judas!" the teacher called. "Judas of Kerioth!"

"Me?"

"Yes, you, my son, and let it be known that Judas of Kerioth was the only one I had to call twice!"

The crowd burst into laughter again as Judas slowly pushed through the crowd until he was standing before Jesus. He knelt. Jesus touched his arm and bid him rise. He gave Judas a bear hug and whispered in his ear.

"Judas Iscariot, I know you. And you will know me."

Jesus drew back and stared at him. The eyes boring into his own blazed with passion—and something else. Judas could have sworn it was pity. The moment passed.

Jesus and Simon made room for him between them, and he took his place and faced the crowd.

"These are my apostles, chosen by my Father—my champions of the Gospel—who will carry it to the uttermost parts of the earth. They will follow me and teach others to follow me. They will heal, preach. And they will suffer. Pray for us and for yourselves."

Suffer? Judas glanced around him at the other eleven, and they looked just as confused as he felt. He shrugged.

All patriots suffer. As long as Rome suffers more—and the Gentiles and Samaritans disappear from the earth—I'm good with it.

***

Leaving Your Lover

Jesus led his newly appointed apostles and the rest of his disciples down the mountain to a wide plain, where they fanned out around him to listen to him speak. Multitudes of people arrived to listen. Judas was awestruck at the power emanating from Jesus. He healed people with his words and his touch. Many people brought their young and their old to be touched, and Jesus healed all who dared approach him.

Now this is a king I can follow. Rome will be no match for him.

Jesus spoke for hours, yet no one wanted to leave. Soon many were sitting or lying on the ground at his feet, listening with rapt attention, shading their eyes against the sun.

He spoke to the poor and the rich, the hungry and the filled, the mourners, the persecuted, the lonely. He spoke about loving and judging—loving your enemies and judging no one because only God has the right to judge another. Judas couldn't quite swallow that, especially the part about loving enemies. How would Rome be conquered by love? The concept baffled him.

Jesus talked about fruit trees and the human heart, sheep and shepherds, kings and peasants. Judas was fascinated by the teacher's ability to move effortlessly from story to point, thrusting it home like a sword to its target.

The carpenter from Nazareth ended his discourse with a lesson about construction, speaking knowledgeably about foundations and where to build the best house. Not, apparently, on the sand. Judas, his mind wandering a bit, was jerked back to the present when he saw Jesus looking directly at him, that sword thrusting home again.

"But anyone who hears and doesn't obey is like a person who builds a house without a solid foundation. When the floods sweep down against that house, it will collapse into a heap of ruins."

As if to punctuate his words, a sudden strong wind blew sand across the throng, swirling in and around the mass of people like a small tornado. It churned around Judas and abruptly stopped, dropping the sand at his feet. He looked down at it, covering his sandals, then looked up, his eyes seeking the teacher's. Jesus had already turned away from him, heading back to Capernaum.

***

Many months later, Judas and Lieber were trailing behind the followers of Jesus as they traveled south from the town of Ephron, or Ephraim, about four miles northeast of Bethel. They had retreated to Ephron after the raising of Lazarus, the miracle that had caught the ear of the religious leaders. After that stupendous show of divine power, those same leaders had vowed to arrest Jesus to prevent Rome from coming down on their heads. Jesus and his disciples were now on their way to Bethany, situated on the eastern slopes of the Mount of Olives, just two short miles from Jerusalem.

Why does he travel toward Jerusalem and those who have vowed to kill him, instead of away? Raising the dead is more provocative than providing food for the hungry or sight to the blind—it was a deeper line in the sand the teacher had drawn, and the religious leaders stood on the other side of it.

Judas looked up and over the heads of those in front of him, just able to see Jesus walking at the head of the procession, his arm around John's shoulder.

He has a death wish, Judas thought angrily.

"What's wrong, Judas? You seem sad these days." Not waiting for an answer, Lieber continued, "Wasn't that breathtaking the way the he answered those Sadducees and Pharisees back there? It seems like he's shut them up for good."

"Hmm…yes, quite."

Lieber prattled on, clearly not noticing the anger mounting on his friend's face.

"It shouldn't be too much longer, I'd say. He'll send Rome packing and break the backs of the religious leaders, and we'll be free of them all. I can't wait to get to Bethany and rest up a bit before it all starts."

No answer from Judas. Lieber shook his arm.

"Judas, aren't you excited?"

Judas stopped and faced his friend, the other disciples flowing around them on the path.

"I'm not so sure the overthrow of Rome is his objective," he said grimly, muscles tense at the thought.

Lieber stared at him, then burst into a tirade. "What? Are you crazy? It's all he's talked about for months! He hates Rome as much as we do, and he calls the religious leaders a brood of vipers. Haven't you been listening?"

"Yes, I have. Have you? I'm hearing something you're not, Lieber."

"Oh yeah? And what might that be?"

"Just watch your back, my friend. Watch your back. And keep your mouth shut and your ears open."

"What do you mean?" Lieber asked incredulously.

"There are subplots churning this night. I heard about a meeting—at the home of that weasel, Caiaphas. The religious leaders are gathering, Lieber. Something's afoot, I tell you."

"So what? They're always up to no good. And where do you come up with this information anyway?"

Judas threw him a pitying glance. "I keep my ear to the ground—as you should, if you want to survive what's coming."

"What's coming? What are you talking about? We already know what's coming."

"A conquering—but not of Rome. And we must choose which side we'll be on when it starts."

"But...we've already..." Lieber sputtered.

Judas laid a heavy hand on Lieber's shoulder.

"My friend, remember his tears as he wept over Jerusalem? I fear he comes not to conquer her Roman masters but to be conquered. Why else does he weep?"

Judas turned his back and continued on the path, leaving Lieber staring after him. Then Lieber charged after him, grabbing his arm from behind, jerking Judas around to face him.

"Judas, you should know what the others say about you."

"I already know. They call me a hypocrite, don't they? They wonder if I'm after the same thing they are. Well, let me tell you, I am. We must be free. The teacher has spoken of freedom, hasn't he?"

Lieber looked down at his feet, then up again, locking eyes with his friend.

"Not that kind of freedom, Judas. He speaks of spiritual freedom, not political freedom."

"So," Judas replied, his eyebrows raised, "you have been listening. And you have made my point quite eloquently. His agenda is not mine."

He turned again and continued walking, Lieber close behind him.

***

Later that evening, having supped with Simon, Jesus reclined at the table, clearly enjoying the company of his good friends. The windows of the house were open, letting in the soft evening breezes and the peaceful sound of chirping cicadas. The room was bathed in the suffused light of the moon peeking through one of the windows and the flickering of small lamps and candles scattered about. It had been a peaceful meal with much laughter, although whenever Judas's eyes met those of Jesus, he saw the curious pity in them.

Into this relaxed, intimate atmosphere crept a woman with an alabaster jar in her hands. Judas supposed she was a serving woman, until the golden moonlight illuminated her face. They were all startled, for she was known to them—Mary, sister of Martha and Lazarus, the same Lazarus whom Jesus had raised from the dead. She quietly approached from behind Jesus and poured the contents over his head and then knelt near his cushion, spreading the perfume over his feet. She stayed with head bowed, fingers clutching the hem of his garment. The rich scent of expensive perfume permeated the room. The men around the table, save the teacher, jumped to their feet in indignation, all speaking at once.

"Here, what is this?

"How dare she?"

"Look at her—she's touching the Master!"

"What a waste! That perfume was worth a year's wages. It should have been sold for a high price and the money given to the poor." Judas's voice rose over the clamor. He was gratified to see that most of the disciples clearly agreed with his assessment.

Jesus raised his hand to stem the flow of angry criticism. He seemed not at all startled or dismayed by Mary's interruption of the evening.

It's almost as if he expected her coming.

"Why criticize this woman for doing such a good thing to me? You will always have the poor among you, but you will not always have me."

Lieber clutched Judas's sleeve.

"She has poured this balm on me to prepare my body for burial. I tell you the truth—wherever the Good News is preached throughout the world, this woman's deed will be remembered and discussed."

Shocked silence followed. Lieber put his mouth close to Judas's ear and whispered, "Burial? What does he mean? He's going to be killed?"

"Shh!" Judas frantically whispered. "Keep your voice down—you're not even supposed to be here!"

Lieber backed away from him, wide eyed. Then he abruptly turned and ran out of the house into the night.

Some semblance of calm was restored as the woman left and the disciples hesitantly resumed their places around the table. No one knew what to say. And Jesus was unhelpful, not explaining his words any further.

Judas, uncomfortable, had lost his appetite for this gathering and finally decided he would go. He wanted to learn what mischief was underway at the home of Caiaphas. If he hurried, he might make it back before the secret meeting disbanded. He stepped out to the porch of the house and paused, gazing into the star-filled sky.

Such peace up there among the stars. Such turmoil down here among men. I wonder why the teacher doesn't just tell us—

"Beautiful, isn't it?" Jesus spoke gently behind him.

Judas, startled, nodded his head. Questions stampeded through his mind, but he couldn't corral any of them.

"Yes, my friend? You have something you want to ask me?"

They stood side by side, the teacher and the taught, as Judas desperately tried to settle on the one question burning in his heart.

How to say it?

He finally decided to just be himself and let the chips fall where they may.

"Teacher, you said you would be buried. I don't understand."

"I know you don't understand. But there's another question, isn't there?"

Judas stared at him as that question finally took solid form in his mind.

"You said 'love your enemies.' How will love conquer the brutish Romans? Are we to lay down our swords and 'love' them to death? Is love now a sharp-pointed weapon to wield, one that will bring Rome to its knees and the corrupt priests along with her?"

Jesus laughed out loud, then placed a tender hand on Judas's shoulder. "Honest to a fault, aren't you? Judas, my son, love is the strongest weapon in the world—if you know how to use it." He added softly, looking up into the night, "And I do." His face glowed in the moonlight.

For a moment Judas thought the light came from within him instead of from above.

"Now, may I ask you a question, Judas of Kerioth?"

Judas nodded, instinctively on guard, muscles tense. Sometimes the teacher's questions were uncomfortable.

"Why do you follow me?"

"Because you called me," he answered immediately, the words sounding pat and false even to his own ears.

"Yes, I called you. My Father chose you. But why do you follow me?"

Judas unexpectedly felt himself anchorless, his mind spinning through possible answers but unable to respond to the simple question. He had no answer. He should have an answer.

It's a simple question. Why do I not have an answer?

The silence stretched. Judas squeezed his eyes shut, hot tears heavy behind his eyelids. The black night became a pit he fell into. It swallowed him whole. He tumbled down into it, turning over and over, frantically reaching to grasp anything to break his fall. But there was only nothingness. In his mind's eye he looked up and saw the loving face of his teacher growing smaller and smaller as he somersaulted into the darkest of gloom. Finally, the shaft into which he'd fallen narrowed until he couldn't see above or below—he only heard the whistling air around him as his body dropped at breakneck speed. He thought his skin must peel off soon. And he knew there'd be no end to the desperate agony in his heart.

His eyes snapped open, and he was alone on the porch. He looked around. Had Jesus just been out here talking to him, or had his tortured mind conjured up the entire conversation?

He slowly turned and opened the door to the house, hearing laughter and camaraderie as the disciples enjoyed the intimate presence of their Master. He hesitated, then let the door close softly.

I don't belong in there. I don't belong anywhere.

His thoughts screamed in anguish as he leaped off the porch and rushed headlong into the dark, back to Jerusalem.

✸✸✸

"Why have you come, Judas Iscariot? Are you not his follower?"

Judas stood in the center of the small, barely lit room in the temple, his face damp in spite of the coolness of the evening. He felt rather than saw the narrowed eyes of ten or twelve religious leaders staring into his own.

Why have I come? Wasn't it to spy on these hypocritical thieves?

Memories of his own thievery drifted across his mind. He thrust that aside and tried to focus on his mission. He must bring about the downfall of these buzzards and their Roman masters. He must force the issue with the teacher. If Jesus were to be caught in a trap, surely he'd fight.

"You are seeking an occasion to trap Jesus of Nazareth. How much are you willing to pay me to set that up for you?"

"And why would you, one of his followers, want to do that? You are disloyal to him? We don't think much of disloyalty in this room, my friend."

The threat wasn't so veiled that Judas didn't hear it. His fear of the power in this room mounted, threatening to overcome him. But it must not. He stilled his trembling hands.

"I am part of his inner circle. He trusts me, so much that I have control of his purse strings."

"And you haven't answered my question," Caiaphas said.

"Why should my reasons matter to you, priest?"

Caiaphas shrugged. "Perhaps it's curiosity. I'm not in the habit of hiring defectors. They can just as easily defect from me. It's not good business."

Judas remained silent.

Caiaphas glanced around at the others. One, Nicodemus, leaned over and whispered in his ear, something Judas couldn't hear. Caiaphas shook his head vigorously, shaking his finger in the other man's face. "No, my friend, we move forward—tonight!"

Nicodemus respectfully bowed his head and moved away from Caiaphas.

"All right, Judas," Caiaphas said. "What's your plan to rid us of this heretic?"

Judas winced inwardly. He knew this was not about religious heresy. No, it was a political game with these priests, and control of the people was their objective.

"I can find out his plans and let you know his movements and where would be the best place to take him. If you'll assign one of these…leaders…as my contact, I can give you time, date, and place." Judas gathered his courage again. "Now, how much will you pay me?"

Caiaphas reached behind him and took a leather bag from the table, holding it out between them. "There are thirty pieces of pure silver in that bag. It's yours. You shouldn't ever have to work again for the rest of your life."

Judas stared at the bag, overcome by the amount offered. Never in his wildest dreams did he think he'd ever have that much money, much less all at once. Still, he hesitated. What he'd agreed to do for it preyed upon his mind in this one moment. He'd spent three years with the man. True, Jesus hadn't yet dispatched Rome's rule as most of them had come to expect, but did he deserve this?

Caiaphas loosened the bag's neck, exposing the silver gleam.

"Well?" the priest demanded.

Judas reached out and took the bag, swiftly tying up the neck once again so as not to spill any.

"This man will be your contact," Caiaphas said, indicating the one to his right. "His name is…well, you can call him Michael."

Judas nodded. "I'll contact you in a day or so. Passover approaches, and he will be busy and probably distracted and unguarded."

Caiaphas stared at him, unblinking. "You may go now. See that you keep your promise. As I said, disloyalty is certainly rewarded in my house."

Judas backed out of the room quickly and hurried out of the courtyard. He felt the eyes of the gate guards on his back as he turned into the street. The jingle of the heavy coin bag did nothing to calm him. In fact, the sound made him feel worse with each footfall.

I'm now a traitor. But perhaps somehow this will come right and will galvanize the teacher to rise up against Rome. Then the rest of us will rally to him.

With these thoughts bringing some small comfort, Judas hurried into the night.

***

A few days later, Judas arrived late at the upper room chosen by Jesus to celebrate Passover with his chosen twelve. As he hurried in, he saw his place across the table from where the teacher reclined. He sat and nervously broke off a piece of the bread on the plate in front of him. John was whispering something to Jesus. They drew apart and laughed, John's eyes crinkling up around his weathered face.

"That was a good story, John. I may use it sometime, with your permission, that is."

John smiled broadly. "You may, Master."

"Stories, I have found, are the best way to tell the truth."

"You have said it, Master," John said, bowing his head in reverence.

Jesus clapped his hands gently then, bringing the disciples to attention.

"Shortly, all that my Father has planned for me will come to pass. But first, there is something that must be done."

Jesus arose, took off his outer garment, and brought a basin of water and a towel to the nearest man and knelt before him. Everyone froze in shock as Messiah washed the grimy feet of Andrew, who wept uncontrollably.

Jesus dried Andrew's feet, then moved to Peter.

"No, you must not wash my feet, Master!"

"You don't understand now, but you will, Peter. If I don't wash you, you will have no part with me."

Peter then cried out, "Then, Master, wash all of me!"

Judas shrank back at this tender intimacy, this abandoned devotion, embarrassed by this emotional display. Hoping Jesus wouldn't notice him, he slowly maneuvered himself back from the table until he was half hidden by the hulking figure of James, the brother of John.

It didn't work. Jesus came last to Judas, kneeling in front of him. He wet the towel and scrubbed vigorously between Judas's toes. Judas thought he would die of shame. He felt the weight of the leather bag at his waist, hidden by his outer cloak.

Jesus looked up into his face. His eyes shone with tenderness and pity.

"Judas, I think your feet are the dirtiest in the room," he said gently, massaging the bottom of his left foot. "Where have you been?"

The others broke out in soft laughter, which angered Judas. His mind scrambled for an acceptable answer. He took a calming breath. "I've been out visiting the poor in the neighborhood," he lied.

"Ahh," Jesus said. "And did you have the coin purse with you to ease their troubled lives?"

Judas jerked his foot slightly.

"What's wrong, my son?"

"You rubbed very hard right there," Judas said, indicating the side of his foot. "I...I...stepped on a rock the other day, and it's still sore. That's all."

"Ahh," Jesus said again. "You must take care where you put your feet, Judas. Watch carefully the path you tread so you don't injure yourself."

"Yes, Teacher."

The uncomfortable conversation came to an end when Jesus stood and resumed his place at the table.

"Please, my friends, eat your fill. Don't be shy. Later, we will go to the usual place of prayer," he announced, looking straight at Judas.

The disciples fell quiet, and for a few moments the only sound was the clink of cups and the scraping of plates.

"I tell you the truth, one of you will betray me," Jesus spoke into the peaceful room.

For the second time that evening, time stopped as everyone froze in shock. Then all the disciples began speaking at once.

"Is it me?"

"Jesus, what do you mean?"

"We'd never betray you. How can you say that?"

"Who is it, Lord?"

The disciples' eyes darted around the room as they asked each other what could be meant by this.

And Judas, knowing he must speak up or be suspected, said also, "Rabbi, am I the one?"

"You have said it," replied Jesus quietly, the pity in his eyes once again. "What you are about to do, do quickly," he whispered, handing Judas a thick piece of bread.

Judas took the bread and ate it. A dark presence, oily and smooth, seeped into his soul as he chewed. He knew that presence. He'd felt it as he tumbled into the imagined pit on the porch in Bethany. Now the blackness of that narrow shaft was part of him, overwhelming him, consuming him. His eyes never left those of Jesus as he swallowed the bread, then stood abruptly.

Going swiftly to the door, he paused with his hand on the rough wood. He turned back to look at Jesus. Their eyes met once again across the dimly lit room. This time, peering through the curtain of that dark presence in his soul, Judas imagined he saw not pity but hatred and condemnation in Jesus's eyes. He dipped his head, jerked the door open, and went out. So be it.

***

Gethsemane filled his nostrils with the spicy scent of the flowering foliage in the garden—purple Na'ah, yellow Ironi-Tzahov, and the blue-pink Achna'i. At any other time he'd enjoy the rich mix of aromas fanned by the night breezes, but tonight it was spoiled by the turmoil in his heart and mind.

He'd left the upper room, and instead of going directly to meet Michael, his contact, he'd come here. He sat on a large flat rock in the center of the clearing. The moon was climbing higher in the sky. In a few minutes it peeked through the canopy and shone directly on Judas, bathing him in a narrow shaft of light. He gazed up at the bright orb, willing the light to give guidance, but the dark presence within wouldn't budge.

It's impossible! My course is set. There's nothing I can do about it now. Yet, perhaps…perhaps…no, it's impossible to change direction now. Caiaphas may have lily-white hands, but the brutes who do his bidding will roast me alive if I back out now.

Humanly speaking, it's impossible. But with God everything is possible.

Judas looked swiftly around, thinking Jesus had followed him here, but he was quite alone. Those were Jesus's words, though, spoken a few days before, just after that hypocritical young ruler had knelt in the dirt at his feet. The words now hung in the air, swirling and echoing around him, bouncing from tree to bush to rock.

He grabbed his head and yanked on his hair at the memory. The words of the teacher, in the beginning, had given rise to much contemplation in his soul, but tonight they could not penetrate the blackness.

I'd best get on with it. They'll be here soon.

Trembling, Judas rose to his feet and hurried out the way he'd come, taking the path to the meeting place with Michael.

***

As Judas and the troop of soldiers rounded the corner into the center of the garden, he was startled to see Jesus kneeling, head down and arms outstretched on the same rock he himself had straddled earlier. He put up a hand to stay the soldiers. They stood silently.

"Father, may this cup pass from me, but nevertheless, your will be done."

The grief in Jesus's voice almost moved Judas, almost penetrated the oily blackness. Almost.

Jesus slowly arose and turned his steps to the small group of sleeping disciples a few yards away.

Judas put a finger to his lips then and waved the soldiers to surround the garden. They obeyed, leaving Judas standing alone. He waited a few moments until he could see the gleam of armor on all sides, then walked purposefully ahead, no longer bothering to hide his presence.

He approached Jesus, who had his back to him, trying to arouse the sleeping disciples.

"Up, my friends! Let's be going. My betrayer is here."

Peter finally stood to his feet. He gently nudged the others until they were awake and rubbing their eyes.

"Master, where are we going?"

Jesus didn't answer immediately, standing silently, still with his back to Judas. Judas had frozen where he was, fists clenched at his sides, thoughts screaming in his head. His tunic was wrapped around him, clinging to him like a shroud. This was the moment. He should rush him, wave the soldiers in, complete the mission. But he couldn't move. He was stuck in this moment, the moment in which his eternity somehow hung in the balance.

He'd almost decided to abandon it, wave the soldiers away, and go to Jesus on his knees. Almost. The clank of a sword on the other side of the grove arrested Peter's attention.

"Master! It's Judas, behind you. Where've you been, man? We've been here for hours!"

Jesus turned to face Judas. The space between them was only a few steps, but it might as well have been a crevasse spanning heaven and hell itself. Silence filled that crevasse for several moments as the two men stared at each other. Judas finally lowered his eyes, hands behind his back.

Leaving Your Lover

His feet finally obeyed him. He went to Jesus, still avoiding his eyes, and kissed him on both cheeks. He felt a curious burning sensation when his lips touched Jesus. He stepped back quickly and glanced around. Soldiers were now filling the spaces between the foliage. The disciples huddled together, clearly afraid and confused.

"My friend, go ahead and do what you've come to do," Jesus said quietly.

Judas beckoned the soldiers to come forward and arrest Jesus. There was a scuffle as Peter attacked one of the high priest's servants, but Jesus subdued him with a gentle admonition. He then bent down and picked up the servant's bloodied ear from the ground at his feet and restored it, all the while looking straight at Judas. Judas looked away, unable to hold Jesus's imploring gaze.

"Get on with it!" he roughly commanded the soldiers.

They took Jesus, bound him, and led him away. The other disciples fled, to a man, and left Judas standing alone beside the rock on which Jesus had prayed.

Judas looked down at the flat surface and saw moisture there. Jesus had shed tears as he'd prayed. Judas stretched out his hand and touched the droplets, startled to feel a tingling in his fingers. Turning his palm over, he was puzzled to see a reddish stain. He brought his hand to his nose and sniffed.

Sweat, and something else. Blood! He'd cried and bled on this rock!

Judas could take no more. He hurried out of that place. He knew what he must do.

Must do…must do…must do.

***

Judas paced outside the room he'd just left. The coin bag felt heavy in his hand.

He'd tried to reason with them, to make them see that he'd meant no harm to Jesus. He'd told them of the miracle Jesus had performed in the garden—the severed ear of the high priest's slave being restored whole—but it seemed only to galvanize their hatred of the teacher.

"I have sinned," he'd declared, trying to escape his own guilt. "For I've betrayed an innocent man."

"What do we care?" they'd declared. "That's your problem."

Blood money, they'd said! How dare they! It was theirs to begin with...and now I can't get the stain of it off my hands.

Judas suddenly stopped in front of the closed door again. He clutched the coin bag between white-knuckled hands. He felt a tickle between his shoulder blades as moisture dripped from the back of his neck. Squeezing his eyes shut, he tried to pray, but the blackness in his mind cloistered the desperate words.

The religious leaders jumped when Judas burst back into the room. They turned as one to face him. Hesitating, Judas stared them down, thinking he would make one more plea to soothe his tormented conscience.

Instead, he gripped the bottom of the heavy coin bag, letting the leather thong loosen as he swung his arm in a wide arc. The heavy coins sprayed the faces of the priests. They put their hands up to protect themselves, but the thick silver coins hit them without warning, clattering to the floor all around them and shimmering under their robes like thirty accusing eyes. The room fell silent as the shocked men stared at him.

Judas dropped the bag, backed out of the room, and ran, leaving the door open. The priests, galvanized to life, crowded the doorway and shouted to the temple guards to apprehend him, but he was already out of sight before they responded.

Twisting and turning down side streets, Judas had no idea where he was going. He finally slowed to a walk, heading north to the Golden Gate and out of the city. He needed to think. To think!

As soon as he was clear of the city, his fogged mind realized he faced the garden where it had all began. He was drawn against his will toward Gethsemane.

He approached again the rock where he'd sat and tried to pray, to justify, to compromise with the God of Israel, where he'd tried to tell God that his motives were pure. He only wanted Israel to be free, to throw off the godless rule of Rome. Messiah had come to do just that. But now Messiah was in chains, headed for the execution stake. He'd never intended that!

Judas stared at the stained rock, then at his stained hands, clutching the rope he'd brought with him. Earlier, he'd tried to wash the stain off, but it seemed to grow darker instead of fading—and the darker the stain grew the darker the presence in his soul became.

For the Son of Man must die, as the Scriptures declared long ago. But how terrible it will be for the one who betrays him. It would be far better for that man if he had never been born!

Judas dropped to his knees before the rock, bowing his head until his forehead rested on the stain, the smell of death filling his nostrils. *He* was that man who wished he had never been born.

He knew what he must do. But first he wanted to just rest here and pretend that this moment was before—before he'd agreed to barter the life of Messiah for a few coins.

Judas kissed Messiah, and the world changed in a blink. He could have changed his mind at any moment and abandoned the path he walked. In this story, Jesus told him to be watchful of the path he trod. He says the same to us.

Our betrayal of Messiah does not happen with a kiss in a garden. It happens each time we turn away from a person in need. It happens when instead of welcoming a newcomer to our fellowship, we skirt them in the lobbies of our churches. Have you ever listened to a sermon, then looked around and applied the teaching to *her*, or to your spouse, to anyone but yourself? We betray Jesus when we don't first see ourselves in God's message.

Each time I gloss over my sin with the attitude that "at least I don't do what *he* does," I betray the One who bled for me on the cross. When I see a single mother or father, and that tiny niggling judgment rises to the surface of my mind and causes me to wonder whose fault it is that there aren't two parents with all those children, I stand judged for my hardhearted attitude.

Jesus calls me to walk the path he walked, with open arms and an open heart to love those he places in my path each day. He calls all of us to gather at the foot of the cross and allow his holy blood to cleanse us, to save us, and to send us out to those who need him.

Is the path you walk today leading you to the betrayer's kiss at the gateway to hell, or to the heavenly gate where Messiah waits to welcome you? There's no time like the present to change directions.

Leaving Your Lover

Think About It...

How have you betrayed your Messiah—to yourself and to those around you? Have you refused to accept the message of salvation, thereby shutting you out of heaven and those for whom you have been given responsibility? Or, if you are a believer, how do you betray him daily by your hardheartedness and pride, causing others to question who he really is?

Will you kneel now and accept his sacrifice on the cross as the only payment for your sin? If you are a believer, will you retrace your steps to the foot of the cross and begin again, repenting of your pride and letting him fill your soul and overflow to those around you?

Chapter 13
Root

For the love of money is the root of all kinds of evil. And some people, craving money, have wandered from the true faith and pierced themselves with many sorrows.
~1 Timothy 6:10

Barnabas the Cypriot silently moved to the front of the assemblage, picking his way through the shoulder-to-shoulder gathering, some standing, some seated on the floor, on tables, wherever they could find a place to sit. He shuffled through the crowd slowly, fists clenched in front of him, face pointed at the rough wooden cross that graced the wall of the small room. He pressed his lids together, tears squeezing out the corners of his eyes and sliding down his weathered cheeks.

The room had grown quiet after Brother Peter had prayed and blessed this gathering of believers in Jerusalem. They'd all been present a few days ago when he and John had returned after being arrested. They'd heard the report of the breathtaking sermon Peter had preached before the entire religious council. They'd waited anxiously, fully expecting the report of their execution, yet here Peter and John now stood before them, bruised and scraped but nevertheless here. The finger of God had moved in their favor. They'd prayed together, felt the shaking of the earthquake, and were filled. Then they also had preached repentance and salvation with great boldness to any who would listen.

And farther back in time, many of this group had witnessed Jesus taken up into the clouds. They had been present when the fire of God's Holy Spirit swept the room in which they met, had looked in awe at the scorching flames on each other's heads. They'd witnessed Peter's sermon to the crowds, the miracles he'd wrought, the healings he'd accomplished.

This hodge-podge of fishermen, tanners, housewives, children, farmers, and metalworkers was the first church formed in Jerusalem after Jesus had gone back to heaven to live with God.

Barnabas now reached the front of the room and fell to his knees before Peter, holding out his gift for the poor. Peter did an astonishing thing. This giant of an apostle, in size and in faith, knelt in front of Barnabas and took his face in his large hands. Forehead to forehead, Peter and Barnabas whispered together, Barnabas finally falling into Peter's arms in a great bear hug.

Peter then stood, grinning ear to ear, and hauled the weeping Barnabas to his feet.

"This son of encouragement has done a beautiful thing here in our midst," announced Peter's great booming voice. "He has sold off one of his fields and has given the money to the poor among us. And he brought ten percent above the price of the field because of his great love for God and for this gathering."

Applause, gleeful shouting, and prayers of thanksgiving mingled together as the people celebrated together. Later, after sharing a simple midday meal together, Peter preached a sermon, encouraging them to keep meeting daily, to love each other, and to share with one another.

The meeting then disbanded. Some left immediately. Others stood around talking in tight knots. Children ran in and out among the adults, screaming with delight. Peter worked the room, shaking hands, encouraging them to live boldly and not to fear.

"Rome can do nothing to us that God does not allow. Remember what Messiah said as he was taken up. We are his emissaries for the Gospel. We must speak it and live it loudly."

Peter worked his way to the back of the room, where a man stood with his wife. She noted his approach and glanced pointedly at her husband. Ananias turned to his wife and took her arm.

As they left the house, she turned a backward glance at the scene still playing out—Barnabas hailed as a hero, red faced with embarrassment at the unexpected attention.

"Brother Barnabas is quite generous, don't you think?" Sapphira asked.

Ananias glanced back with a scowl on his face.

"So it would seem, wife."

"And he a Levite—they are not to own property in Israel. So what is this about him selling a piece of land? Seems suspicious to me," she said with a touch of asperity.

"I heard the property is actually in Cyprus, inherited from his family. I overheard him the other day telling Peter that he would donate it because as a Levite he couldn't keep it."

Sapphira sniffed haughtily.

"As you say, husband. I think he's got something up his sleeve. Still, I would think Peter would not allow such hero worship of one man. I thought it was God we are to worship."

Ananias did not answer her.

She studied his face as they slowly made their way through the mean streets to their own neighborhood. Worry lines etched his forehead, his gray beard was thinner each year, and his heavy-lidded eyes had developed pouches. No matter. She loved this man with a passion rarely exhibited to others. It had set her on fire three decades ago when she'd first met him.

He had called on her father, ostensibly to ask a question about sheep, but, really! She'd known what was happening, and it had caused her heart to almost fail in her chest. Furtively watching them out the door of their small home, she'd taken in every inch of him. She'd liked what she'd seen then, at age fourteen, and she still did. She'd had to fight off others in her circle of friends—equally inflamed by him and older and more beautiful than she—and she'd let them know in no uncertain terms he would be hers. She'd never regretted it.

When they reached their home in the more affluent part of the City of David, they made their way to their upper sanctuary to talk over what was happening in the fledgling church.

Sapphira waved her women away, flocking around her like so many hens.

"Leave us," she said imperiously. "I will call you later."

"Mary." She called the youngest one back. "Bring our account scrolls. Not the shop ones—the property ones." She turned away as Mary scurried off to do her bidding.

"What's on your mind, wife? Are we behind in our bookkeeping? Or do you want to see if we're being bilked by that new accountant?"

"No, although he bears watching after what I heard at the market the other day from the potter. He had it from a traveler that—" She broke off as Mary came in with the land account scrolls.

"I'm going to go change. I'll be right back," Ananias said, heading for his own rooms.

"Thank you, Mary," Sapphira said, taking the scrolls. "You may go. See that the evening meal preparations are progressing as they should. And I want you serving at table this evening. It's high time you learn something besides washing pots."

She ignored Mary's squeal of delight. She flicked a hand in her direction, and Mary left quickly, no doubt to brag to the other servants about her elevated status. Sapphira forgot her as soon as she was out of sight.

She removed her outer wrap, shook her luxuriant dark hair out of its bejeweled restraints, and sat down at the ornate desk Ananias had bought recently from a Sidonian trader. He'd presented it to her on the occasion of their latest land acquisition.

She ran her hand over the smooth cedar polished to a high sheen, enjoying the sensual feel of such opulence. Not even her father, who'd told her when she was fourteen that he had a feeling Ananias would go far, could have known how well they'd be sitting today.

Ananias stepped back into the room, divested of his formal robes and dressed in the casual tunic he wore only at home. He stepped to her side and placed a large hand on the back of her neck, massaging gently. Her thick hair fell to her waist. Leaning down, he kissed the top of her head. Then he knelt next to her, a gleam in his eye.

"Not now, Ananias. We have work to do," she said, gently pushing him away.

He laughed, taking her chin in his fingers. "Work? What work, my sweet?"

"I've been thinking."

"As usual." He stood and stepped around to the other side of her desk and sat facing her.

"Now don't tease me, husband. We enjoy a certain status in the city, do we not?"

"Yes. So what? We've worked hard for it."

"Perhaps we should broaden our horizons."

"What do you mean?"

"Respect can be bought in other places than in the Jerusalem marketplace, husband."

Ananias reached for the scroll she had in front of her. She'd been studying a parcel of land to the east of the city that had been owned by her family for generations and had come into her possession upon the death of her father two and a half years ago. Ananias looked up at her, clearly puzzled, and waved the scroll in her face.

"All right, spill it, Sapphira. What are you plotting?"

She took the scroll back from him, spreading it out between them on the desk.

"What do you think this land is worth?" she asked, stabbing it with her finger. The rings on her hands glittered in the late-afternoon sunlight streaming through the window.

"I'm not sure. Certainly more than your father paid for it."

"Perhaps you should find out. Ask around, but with discretion. I don't want everyone in Jerusalem to know our business."

"If you say so. I can do that tomorrow—put some feelers out. But why? Are you thinking of selling it? I thought we agreed we would hold it for a while, let it increase a bit more in value. We've only owned it for a couple of years. Why not just sit on it?"

"I think the time has come. And it's my land to do with as I see fit—isn't that right?" she challenged.

"Yes, yes, of course. But you still haven't told me why."

"All in good time, husband. Just let me know what you find out."

She rolled up the scroll, fastened it, and laid it gently in the box with all the others.

"Now, I must go see to the kitchen servants. I will see you at dinner." She turned her back on him and walked swiftly to the door.

"You'll go tomorrow? I want no delay."

"Yes, of course. I told you I would," he replied, clearly rankled by her domineering tone.

She stared at him a moment longer, then went out. She descended three levels to the kitchens, her severe expression causing servants to scatter before her. Her mind worked furiously as her ambitious plan churned.

Ananias, it's for you I do this. Always for you. It's as much for your dignity and prestige as mine—nay, more. For when you rise in public opinion, so do I. My love, you have no idea the lengths I've gone to, and will in the future, to assure your success.

***

Leaving Your Lover

The next day, Ananias arrived home late in the afternoon. He found Sapphira instructing a new maid in the fine arts of laundering. Sapphira immediately knew he had news for her, so she shooed the maid away. As she scuttled out with a relieved expression on her face, Ananias chuckled.

"Finally, you're home. I've been on pins and needles, waiting for you."

"I see you're making a new friend, my dear wife," he said, giving her a kiss on the cheek.

"Yes, well, I don't know who trained her before I bought her, but whoever it was knows nothing about how a servant should respond to her mistress. But enough of that. What news?"

"I did as you asked me to. I found three who are interested in the land."

"You were discreet, husband?"

"Very. They won't talk."

She rubbed her hands together. "What was the highest price offered?"

He told her, and her eyes sparkled.

"Let's accept that bid, husband. Can you contact him again today?"

"What's your hurry? I can track him down tomorrow if you like."

"Today…it must be today. And I want the money in our hands today. Do you think that's possible?"

His eyebrows climbed up his forehead as his eyes widened in surprise. "Why? Isn't it enough we've been promised three times what we expected?" He leaned over and tapped her forehead with his forefinger. "What is going on up there, my devious wife? I can tell you have some plan cooking. When are you going to tell me?" He grabbed her elbow gently and drew her to him. "Or do I have to beat it out of you?"

She turned startled eyes on his face. What she saw there allayed her fears. She pushed him away.

"Enough of your playing. There will be time enough for that—later. Now listen and I'll tell you what we'll be celebrating at this time tomorrow."

***

"You're sure, my friend? There's no mistake?"

"Positive. I was in the market today, and I overheard the entire conversation. That is the price offered for the property. And they shook on it. Do you realize what this could mean?"

"Yes, John, I do. Many of our poorest will be fed for quite a while," Peter said, hands folded in front of him. "Praise God, who supplies everything we need."

John nodded. "Indeed, brother. When can we tell the others?"

Peter laid a calming hand on John's arm. "No, we must wait. It's not our news to share. Are you positive that they intend to donate the proceeds? They don't have to, you know, and frankly, it surprises me that they would."

"Yes, it surprised me to hear it. They haven't exactly been closely involved with our company—more like observing from the fringes. But it sounds like that is their intent." John grinned. "It sounds like God is speaking to them, doesn't it?"

"We'll see, my friend. But this news is encouraging, certainly. We'll see what develops. We may be celebrating God's provision again, and soon."

***

The next day when the believers met, as they had been daily since Messiah had been taken up, Peter delivered a powerful lesson on the subject of hypocrisy. His lesson followed that of Messiah's, who spoke many times about the hypocrisy of the religious leaders.

"But it wasn't just a denouncement of our leaders, my good friends. He spoke to us, warning us over and over that our motives for following him must be pure, untainted by worldly passions."

Leaving Your Lover

Ananias and Sapphira were again among the company, this time standing closer to the front of the group. They listened quietly, nodding their heads with the others as Peter rammed home his application.

"For instance, our Lord said of our leaders, 'Everything they do is for show.' He called them 'whitewashed tombs' and 'blind guides.' How much more are we when we follow their example? We look like them when we practice their 'religion'—beautiful on the outside but filled on the inside with dead people's bones."

By now some were weeping, kneeling at Peter's feet, retching out their repentance and receiving his warm hand on their heads.

"My good people, I don't want to bring sorrow upon sorrow to you. Submit yourselves to God. Follow him alone, in purity of love and motive. Love others as yourselves, nay, more than yourselves, and he will draw you close. Give up your treasure on this earth to gain the treasure stored up for you in heaven."

Peter then knelt in front of the small group of prostrate believers, soothing and comforting them. Soft weeping could be heard in all corners of the room.

Ananias and Sapphira, still standing in the center of the room, picked their way through the crowd and crept quietly away. As they gained the street, Sapphira took a deep breath and squared her shoulders. She looked down and flicked a speck of dust from her luxurious bodice, then picked up the hem of her dress and shook it out.

"Peter's very adamant these days. He seems to have a one-track mind. Husband, don't you think it's possible to be rich and comfortable *and* a follower of Messiah? I don't remember him preaching that having wealth is inherently evil. Do you?"

"No, I can't say that I do." He studied his wife's discontented face. "Are you thinking of the donation of the price for our land?" Seeing her sharp glance, he added, "Your land?"

"Yes, I am. There is no reason we have to give away all of it. It's ours to do with as we please. They should be grateful they're getting any of it."

"Hmm. One would think Peter's words caused you to feel guilt over it."

"I am not guilty of anything, husband, except excessive generosity toward those followers who, for one reason or another, refuse to work for a living. As I said, they should feel grateful that they're provided for. And on the morrow, they will have more reason to feel grateful."

Ananias grinned. "And it won't do us any harm either, will it? The respect we will garner will surely make next year's business profits soar."

With that, they continued to their home, where they expected to meet shortly with the buyer of their property.

***

"Ananias, my friend! How are you this good day? I enjoyed seeing you and your lovely wife at the gatherings this week." Peter shook the other man's hand, noting the heavy leather pouch he carried at his side.

"My brother, I am fine. God be praised, he provides mightily for us, does he not?"

"Indeed he does. But what brings you here at this hour? There is no meeting planned for today."

"I wanted a private moment with you, sir. No need to make this a big show." He handed the leather bag to Peter.

"But what's this?" Peter peered into the bag.

"Sapphira sold a piece of her father's property. It's a goodly size, worth someone cultivating some crop or other. In fact, the buyer intends to do just that, and make a handsome profit, I'll warrant."

Peter beamed at him. "And this, this is a donation to our body of believers?"

Ananias waved a hand, assuming a humble manner, looking straight into Peter's eyes.

"Yes, it's the least we can do. We live comfortably and make a profit each year with our business interests. We decided it's

time to invest in God's kingdom. We promised God that whatever we received for the land, we would give all to the poor."

"You don't know how this encourages me, brother!" Peter clapped Ananias on the shoulder. "How much did you get for the land, if I may ask?" He eyed the contents of the bag again.

"That's all of it, right there in that bag." He named the price.

"But..." Peter started. He felt the weight, mentally measuring the contents once again, then narrowed his eyes as he looked at Ananias.

Ananias took a step back, nearly knocking over a small table behind him.

"This can't be the entire price, Ananias." Peter's voice was harsh.

"But it is. We took quite a beating—we could have kept it for a few years and sold it for much more. But the poor need it now."

Peter shoved the money bag back into Ananias's hand. "Ananias, why have you let Satan fill your heart? You have lied to me, and you kept back some of the money for yourself. Admit it!"

"Why, how dare you accuse me of lying!"

"The property was yours to sell or to keep. And after you sold it, you could have kept some of it for yourself. But to lie about it! You weren't lying just to me, but to God!"

Ananias let go of the bag, and it thudded to the floor, the coins rolling around Peter's feet. His eyes bulged, and he clutched his chest with his right hand, a purple hue creeping up his neck and spreading over his face. He coughed then—a heavy, deep cough that brought forth a stream of red mucous that covered his mouth and flowed down his chin. He frantically stretched out his other hand toward Peter. Peter took his arm but was unable to keep him from crumpling to the floor. Ananias was dead before he hit the ground.

Peter stepped to the doorway and motioned to two young men.

"Ananias has collapsed and died. Please take him out and bury him."

The two men picked him up by his shoulders and feet and took him out. Peter stared after them, a tear slipping down his cheek. He picked up the spilled coins and replaced them in the bag, which he put on a small table. He heard a sudden sound behind him. Fully expecting to see Sapphira there, he rotated swiftly, but was surprised to see John.

He rushed into the room, face aghast at the bloody mess at Peter's feet. He turned suspicious eyes on his friend.

"Brother, what happened? I just saw the body of Ananias carried through the street."

"God has judged him. I didn't lay a hand on him. You know I wouldn't."

"Yes, of course, Brother. But what happened?"

"John, he tried to trick us! The amount he brought," he said, gesturing to the bag behind him, "is nowhere near the amount you heard discussed."

John looked into the bag, hefted it in his hands, and put it gently back on the table. He turned troubled eyes to Peter.

"Maybe he changed his mind. Maybe they needed part of the money."

"No, I asked him point blank what price he received for the land, and he lied about it. He told me the full price of the land is in that bag."

"It can't be. It's much less. But why would he do that? We'd have been glad for any amount he'd cared to donate." He stopped, a look of consternation on his countenance. "Do you suppose Sapphira knows what he's done?"

Peter put a gentle hand on John's shoulder. It was obvious to Peter that John, known for his deep love for others, now carried a broken heart. Peter sympathized, but he was much more concerned for the reputation of Messiah and the church.

"John, I don't know if she's aware. I'll wager we'll find out before this day is done. Perhaps you would care to go and supervise the burial—make sure they do it correctly. And we must keep it quiet until I speak to Sapphira. I'm going now to try to find her."

John went out, looking like the world sat on his bowed shoulders.

Peter spent the afternoon looking for Sapphira. He went to her house, but she was not there, nor did the servants know where she'd gone. He wandered the market, but didn't see her. Finally, he went back to the meeting place to wait.

She'll arrive soon, I have no doubt, especially if she gets wind of the events this day.

About three hours later, Sapphira came in. Peter stood immediately and greeted her warily.

"Have you seen my husband, Brother Peter? He was coming to see you earlier, but that was hours ago. Did he arrive?"

She doesn't know.

"Yes, he arrived." He picked up the bag of silver and held it in front of him.

"Oh, good! He gave it to you. My father would be so happy to know that his land helped feed our poorest brothers and sisters."

"I wasn't aware that your father cared so much for the poor," Peter answered.

"Well, he generally didn't like to make a show of it, but he did—he cared deeply."

"Like you and your husband, Sapphira?" Peter's voice had flattened, his lips no longer smiling.

Sapphira was clearly alert now, a calculating expression stamped on her face.

"Why, Peter, are you trying to say something to me? If so, just say it. These veiled criticisms are beneath you, as one of Messiah's apostles."

Peter started to retaliate, but thought better of it. Instead, he handed her a slip of paper on which he'd written the full sum Ananias had told him they'd received.

"Tell me, is that the full price you received for your father's property? And is that full price here in this bag?"

Sapphira hesitated. "Yes," she finally said, "that was the price."

Peter took the paper out of her hand, put it into the bag of silver, and set the bag down on the floor between them. Sapphira looked down at the bag, then up at Peter.

"But, what are you…" Her calculating expression now dissolved into fear.

"How could the two of you even think of conspiring to test the Spirit of the Lord like this?"

Sapphira stumbled backward at Peter's severe pronouncement. Then she straightened again, clearly gathering herself to challenge him.

"How dare you…" She got no further.

"Where is your husband, you ask? The young men who buried him three hours ago are just outside the door, and they will carry you out too!"

Sapphira's eyes dilated in terror. Then she fell straight forward, landing with a dull thud at Peter's feet, her head bouncing once. One hand stretched out feebly and clutched at the bag. She died there, fingers wrapped around the bag of silver.

By that time the next day, the entire Jerusalem church knew what Ananias and Sapphira had planned. Word of their dramatic deaths reached every corner of the city and beyond. Tongues chattered about it for days afterward. Peter spoke about it, warning his little flock about the consequences of such hypocrisy. And great fear gripped the entire church and everyone else who heard what had happened.

The root of evil, this love of self and money, caused the flowers to bloom above their graves, reminding all of us from that time to this that we cannot hide hypocrisy and God will not be mocked.

Love of money, self, and status is as insidious as the disease that invades our physical bodies with no immediate symptoms. We don't know it's there until it is too late. It silently travels the bloodstream, conquering cell after cell, weakening us as we go about our business. We think we have forever, but unknown to us our time is short. One day, the specialist gives the bad news that it's time to talk about end-of-life issues.

If this spiritual disease is not recognized and eradicated, it destroys as surely as the invader in our bodies. And it does not confine itself to those who have large bank accounts. It manifests itself in the most innocent of places.

It's in our workplaces, as we jockey for position, stepping on others to move just one level up. It invades our churches, as we peer down our noses at those "different" from us, those less fortunate, those who don't pray with just the right spiritual words. And it is a destroyer of families. We judge each other for the least infraction, severing relationships over the feeblest of reasons, carry grudges going back decades, even to the point that we don't remember why we were angry in the first place.

Brothers and sisters, this must not be. We must put this disease to death, or one day we will wake up to the smoldering ruins of our lives. If Ananias and Sapphira could communicate with us from eternity, be assured they would tell us to be careful, that God knows our hearts and that he *will* glorify himself—as on the day they both died at Peter's feet

Think About It...

How have you lied to God? Have you made promises to him you have no intention of keeping? Are you a hypocrite, pretending to love God at church but looking down your nose at others during the week? Is there a group of people who you think does not deserve God's mercy?

Will you choose integrity even when it hurts? Will you see others, no matter who they are or what they've done, the way God sees them—as worth the price of his Son?

Previous Books by Deb Gorman

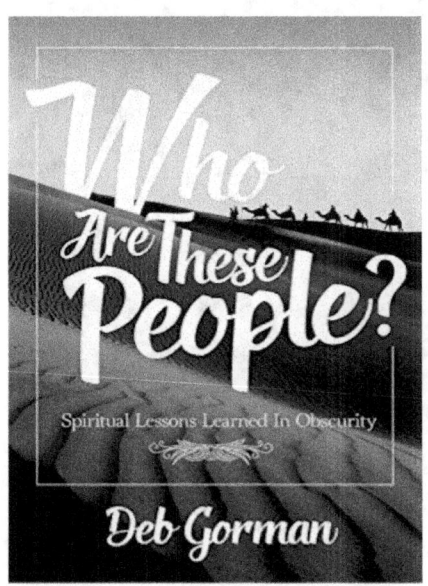

Encountering Jesus amid our flawed lives, we discover He is bigger than our rebellion, our tragedies, and our confusion.

This devotional plunges you into the lives of twelve biblical characters who are mentioned briefly, almost parenthetically, as the stories of well-known players are told. Several of these obscure individuals aren't even named. But God included them in His Word for a reason, and the reason is us. Author Deb Gorman puts flesh on the bones of these shadow people, to name them, to fill in the canvas of their lives so spiritual truths can be extracted.

So, get ready to meet these personalities in a new way. And the next time you're tempted to think your life is insignificant, that God can't use such a flawed, mistake-ridden person such as yourself, remember: these twelve people probably thought the same, and here you are reading their stories and learning powerful lessons from their encounters with God. God created you to impact others, and that is definitely not insignificant!

The path of your life will change each time you hold fast to your faith.

This book is about choices. If there is one thing universal in the human experience, it's that we make choices every day.

Our choices range from determining how much we'll spend for a cup of coffee to whom we'll spend the rest of our lives with, but only one choice determines where we'll spend eternity.

This devotional immerses you into the lives of six Biblical characters whom God brought to the sharp point of radical decisions—decisions that would change the course of their earthly existences.

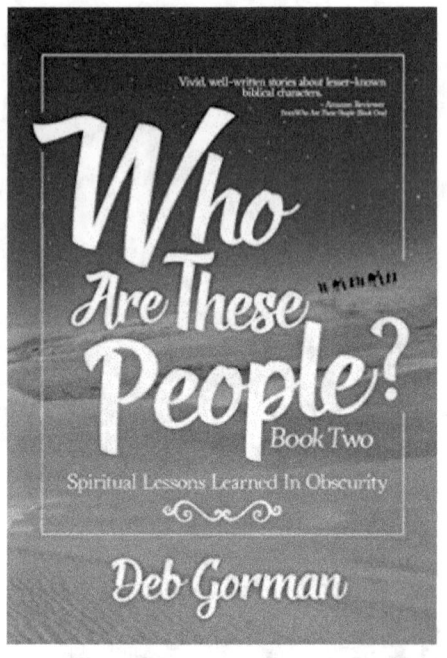

We might think these six people have nothing to do with us in our century of instant communication, driverless cars, and computers mounted on our wrists, but the earth is old, and humankind hasn't changed. The choices we make each day still determine the next moment, the next year, the next millennium and have far-reaching consequences for the next generation. God included these characters in His Word for a reason, and the reason is us.

www.ingramcontent.com/pod-product-compliance
Lightning Source LLC
Chambersburg PA
CBHW070758020526
44118CB00036B/1890